About The Author

Margot Cairnes has been working in the field of strategic change with top organisations in both Australia and overseas for the past seven years. After graduating from Sydney University as the first University Medallist in her field, Margot worked as the Chief Executive of a group of companies before completing an MBA and lecturing in Organisational Change, Politics and Sociology at Sydney University, the University of the Northern Territory and the Macquarie Graduate School of Management. She then worked as a senior partner in the Strategic Consulting Group before setting up her own company, The Change Dynamic.

Margot writes regularly on management, communication, change and relationships. She has appeared on both radio and television and is featured in the ABC book *The Search for Meaning II*. Her client list includes top international and national financial, management, government, corporate and educational institutions.

Margot lives in Sydney with her husband and two children.

Peaceful Chaos

The Art Of Leadership In Time Of Rapid Change

Margot Cairnes

The Change Dynamic

First published in 1992 by The Change Dynamic
PO Box 961
Neutral Bay   2089
Telephone: 962 9701

To protect the anonymity of my clients, I have changed names, key facts and
any identifying features in the case studies used in this book. While I have maintained the
essence and integrity of the work and people involved,
the individuals cited are fictitious.

Printed by Shepson Printing Pty Ltd
Bound by Les Baddock & Sons Pty Ltd

I dedicate this book to my late father, Alan Cairnes, who taught me through his actions that to live a lie is killing, while to live your truth is to unleash your talents, wisdom and inner peace.

Acknowledgements

Despite having read thousands of books I have never realised until I wrote one how many people are involved in the process of formulation, writing and publication. A book is a joint effort.

I therefore take this opportunity to thank my husband, Christian Muzard, for his encouragement, support and understanding; without him I would never have started.

I thank my children, Lija and Andrew, for their patience and resourcefulness in managing without me while I stayed glued to my computer.

I thank my clients for their faith, trust and courage, while we navigated new waters. I also thank my staff Liska Reinstorf, Ian Hayes and Margaret Coleman, and my editor Margaret Jones, for their patient effort and support in preparing the manuscript for publication.

Finally, I thank my teachers and friends for their support, challenge, guidance and love.

Contents

Foreword

'Be the best in the world at what you do or you will go out of business.'

That simple and straightforward message is reverberating through the halls of Australian industry. In some cases it's too late; the alarm bells are echoing in empty factories and offices.

It's not that we don't know what must be done. The need for dramatic change to revitalise Australia's sluggish industrial performance has been widely discussed and acknowledged by industry, government, and unions alike. But change is coming painfully slowly. Too slowly.

It is no time to panic, yet it is all too easy to panic as the need for decisive action becomes increasingly more urgent. As time grows shorter and the list of things that need to be done grows longer it is often possible to feel that the walls are closing in. Claustrophobia is the enemy of rational thought.

So space is a valuable commodity. Space to reflect on strategies and their possible outcomes. Space to scan the distant horizon for threats and opportunities. And space to look deeper for the blockages that are limiting our success.

In my opinion, individual and collective fear of change is proving to be a major blockage we face. It takes many forms. Fear of losing jobs, of losing status, of risking career prospects. Fear of rebuke from superiors for making a mistake. Fear of ridicule from peers for making an off–the–wall suggestion for improvement. Fear of allowing subordinates to grow in case they should excel and displace those above them. Fear of delegation in case it leads to unsatisfactory work and subsequent retribution.

We are a nation which is more likely to take steps to cover its backside than it is to take risks in pursuit of quantum gains. Fear is capable of motivation. But it is incapable of personal empowerment and, in many ways, we are using fear to try to achieve this.

I'm certain that, if we look at those sections of industry where we have made quantum improvements we'll find that the people involved were empowered, in part, through the removal of fear.

I know from experience that significant improvements have been made by people who have no fear of trial and error in pursuit of the objective that has been set. They'll happily talk about their failures and what they learned from them. They are thriving in an environment that supplants the fear of failure with the joy of success.

When we have a critical mass of people who feel that way, I'm confident that we'll see our results improving.

But we'll only see that critical mass develop individual by individual. We all have our own fears. They all have to be addressed in their own way; there's no magic formula, no standard operating procedure for removing them. That's why I believe that, as managers, we must turn our attention to addressing the concerns of each individual within our organisation.

The benefits of doing that within my own organisation are beginning to become apparent; in several aspects of our operation we have already become the best in the world.

There's no end point, of course. We are, and always will be, confronted by the need to improve at a greater rate than our competitors. But it's becoming clearer every day that we're on the right track. By addressing the needs of the individual we're bringing greater productivity to the organisation and opening up a whole new dimension to our lives.

As for a starting point, it's obvious to me now—it wasn't for many years—that the first individual that we need to work with is ourselves.

As managers we've been exhorting others to change but, at the same time, we've been fearful of letting go the old ways on which we've based our authority, influence and self–esteem. If we are to be successful in the future, those old ways have to go because they are holding others back from realising their full potential. Admitting that we are the ones creating the blockage is the first step—and the most difficult.

And that's where Margot's book can provide useful and powerful support. Margot reinforces the wisdom of working with the individual instead of the faceless collective. She offers a guiding light and the stimulation to begin your own journey into your own space, and the encouragement to continue down a path that will lead to great personal reward and satisfaction.

From such journeys might well come the ability for Australia to put aside its fear of failure and ride high on the joy of success.

David Judd
Portland
February 1992

Chapter 1

Combining Personal Well–Being With Worldly Success

Meet William Webster. You have probably read about him. He is a public figure of some note. He leads in his field. He is affluent and influential. You may have seen him driving around in his late-model BMW.

William's attractive wife, Susan, is often in the social pages. A little less now because as the children are older she has started up her own successful retailing business. The three Webster children are a source of pride to their parents. They are all in the best schools, the boys are good at sport and Sally, the youngest, is very artistic.

The Websters' home is magnificent. They bought an older style house some years ago at what turned out to be a bargain price. It needed a lot of work but they fell in love with the view and the area in which the house is situated. Susan took out a builder's licence and supervised the renovations. She did a great job. Their home was featured in *Home Beautiful*.

Everybody wonders how they achieve so much. William plays off an 8 handicap at golf, Susan is treasurer of the Mothers' Club at two schools, they often entertain, and then there's that wonderful weekender of theirs. William has become a bit portly, while Susan is a regular at the local gym and looks as slim and fit as ever. The whole family is always beautifully dressed.

Yes, the Websters appear to have it all. They are the kind of people we write, read and talk about. It is the Websters and their kind that we admire, envy and strive to emulate.

William Webster is one of my clients. I have the privilege of working with William and many like him who lead in various areas of public life. I'm an organisational change agent. I specialise in helping leaders introduce change into their businesses, government departments, professional practices and community organisations.

Change is all about people, and people aren't always what they seem to be. When I first started my work I was amazed that people like William needed help. They seemed to have everything going for them already, but the closer I got to very successful people and the more I learned about change, the more I realised that maybe William didn't have everything after all. Perhaps there was something missing.

The missing something

William had it all but he was rarely home to enjoy his attractive wife, his magnificent house or his pride–giving children. William was always working. Even when he played golf it was to build his network or cement a deal. He was always busy, always on the move and always preoccupied. He showed up at the dinner parties, at the beach house and at family occasions, but generally his relationships were long–distance. Even when he was with people he cared about he was unable to establish any emotional closeness.   William was so busy thinking about what he wanted to achieve and how he was going to achieve it that he was rarely available to enjoy any of the many pleasures in his life.

His constant non-availability was creating problems for William both at home and at work. His marriage was distant and lonely. Everything looked great but he felt alone, misunderstood and bored. He loved his wife and children but hated their demands, and deep inside, if he dared to admit it, he resented the demands of earning the money, spending the time and going through the motions of keeping the family in luxury.

At work his constant striving for increased success was affecting both his relationships with and the effectiveness of the people around him. It seemed to William that everywhere he looked people worked according to hidden political agendas that didn't accord with what he thought was best practice. Moreover, it seemed that office politics consumed so much of his time he wasn't able to achieve what he thought was reasonable.

His staff found him an exacting boss. No matter how much they gave, he wanted more; nothing was ever good enough. They found him difficult to 'get through to' and were unable to explain to him the very real problems they felt they were facing in their work. William was continually frustrated because he was unable to achieve what he knew was possible.

William had lived with these 'irritations' for some time — he had contacted me because he wanted to implement a new strategy into his organisation and was having difficulty getting people to change their attitudes and their behaviours. Publicly, everybody agreed the changes seemed reasonable, but he sensed there was a lot of passive resistance and the change was 'taking too long'. He thought I might be able to help get his people 'to own the changes'.

Unlike many successful leaders, William was able to see that he might be part of the problem. As we worked together on the environmental changes and the attitude change in his people, William began to realise that a large part of his discomfort and many of their problems with acceptance of the proposed changes stemmed from him.

Early learning

William had learned early that success was a way to get other people's approval.   The more he learned about himself, the more William realised that a large part of his behaviour was motivated by gaining the approval of others.   At the same time, however, his constant striving for success kept him apart from the very people he wanted to impress.   He rarely relaxed, didn't really trust people and was worried that should he fail he would be rejected by his peers and his family.   William's success was largely driven by fear of rejection.   That same fear kept him from enjoying what he had achieved and from cultivating meaningful relationships.   In his constant, if unconscious, attempt to gain others' approval, William had lost the ability to gain his own approval.   He was a very hard and exacting taskmaster to himself.   He rarely stopped to notice how he felt, what he wanted for himself or what would make him happy. His focus remained on achieving goals.   The people around him had begun to resent his single-mindedness and felt that they were merely instrumental to William's 'grand plans'.

After I had worked with William and his top team for over a year, William began to experience the support and goodwill that go with growing emotional intimacy.   He began to take more responsibility for his own well-being and realised that in so doing he lost nothing of his effectiveness and in fact gained increased effort and contribution from those around him.

One day he told me, 'I knew there was something missing, but I didn't know what it was. Since I've been doing this work I've come to realise that what was missing was me.' In his search for success William had put aside his own capacity to feel, to fully experience his life and to get in touch with his own inner wisdom. In so doing he had lost the most valuable of life's gifts — the ability to be true to himself, to enjoy his life and to live in peace.

The role of socialisation in our success

Unfortunately many of us have given up 'ourselves' to become successful. In fact in many cases the more successfully we have been able to deny our own feelings and inner wisdom, the more successful we have become.

Technically, the process of giving up our own identities is called socialisation. It is the process by which children learn to deny their own drives and needs and become a 'functioning' part of society. It is through socialisation that we learn to fit into a family, a school, a community and later a work environment. The more successfully we are socialised, the more successful we are likely to become in a society which rewards people for their ability to behave in socially sanctioned ways. Each culture has its own ways of socialising its members. Each way has its benefits and its problems.

In our culture, the way we have socialised children has allowed us to build a civilisation that is more innovative and advanced than any before it. We have developed complex world-wide organisations and political systems and have created highly sophisticated and rapidly changing technologies that have allowed us to explore outer space, feed our rapidly growing population, achieve medical miracles and find computer applications that have revolutionised every form of work and private life.

Our processes of socialisation have created people who can

live, work and manage others in an age of information explosion. We have learnt to look outside ourselves for challenges, new information and answers to a wide and varied range of issues and problems. As a society we are very problem and solution focused.

We learnt this early. We learnt that if we did what our parents or caregivers wanted we were rewarded with attention, love or treats. If we didn't do what the big folk thought we should we were usually punished by withdrawal of love, privilege or freedom. We were sent to our room, frozen out or denied involvement in some favoured activity.

In each home the system of rewards and punishments and the criteria on which they are given out is different, but in every home the process of socialisation goes on. It's the way that adults manage to live with the children they raise and how children learn to fit in. Those of us who are well socialised are those who know how to become successful, contributing members of society.

What socialisation left out

Increasingly, we learn from the fields of psychology and psychotherapy that sound emotional health is based on the individual's ability to think for themselves, to follow their own intuition and instincts and to fully experience their own sense of being, even when it is at odds with what others dictate. To be a successfully functioning human being is to fully experience your own emotional reality, to trust your own guidance, to follow your own path and thus to be self–determining. To do otherwise is to risk mental disorder, stress, emotional and physical breakdown and a lifetime of alienation from yourself and others. In social terms these symptoms emerge as crime, social and family breakdown, emotional and physical violence and a whole range of illnesses such as drug and alcohol dependence, psychosomatic disorders, workaholism and phobias of every sort.

The same socialisation process that taught us to look outside ourselves for guidance as to what was appropriate behaviour has taught us to deny our own emotions, intuition and well-being. We have been taught that success is determined by the approval of others. We thus measure success in terms of visible things such as a good job, a good-looking spouse, gifted children and material wealth. We see success as doing well at exams, achieving business goals and attracting public acclaim. While we pay lip service to happiness, family life and relationships, we tend to judge our success in all these areas by what looks good rather than by how we feel. Emotions are intangible and 'soft' and we accord them less importance than external appearances. Many of us have forgotten the human gifts of experiencing life in our own unique, way as our own person complete with emotions, a rich spiritual life and the zest and courage to seek and follow our own lead.

Enter rapid change

A system of socialisation based on external sanctions teaches us to put our centre of decision-making and power outside   ourselves. Our decision-making criteria become dependent on the approval and reactions of others. In simple systems and at times of moderate change we can afford the luxury of playing the games of politics and approval-seeking. We can abdicate power and responsibility for our well-being, our decision-making and our success to others. We can get to know the stable players and situations in our life, and learn who and what we need to influence and how we can best do it. Life is simple: we all know the games we are playing. Winning means playing better than anyone else.

Enter rapid change.   The scientific revolution known as Chaos Theory has shown us that all systems are inherently unstable. The more complex the system, the more unstable it is.   Due to this instability even the smallest change in any part of a system can lead to rapid change, even revolution, in another part of the system.

We can see this in the recent, rapid changes in eastern Europe.   We also experience it in physical systems such as the weather, where it is reputed that a butterfly flapping its wings in one part of the world can lead to a tornado somewhere else.

Change, instability and chaos are the norm, not a temporary aberration. The only constant is change. We are born, mature and die. Change is part of the definition of life. The only thing of which we can be absolutely sure is that things will change.

Our society, being so complex, is very susceptible to change. New information, changing relationships and the rise and fall of governments and organisations all ensure that change is ever with us and always increasing.   We are experiencing family breakdown, company start-up and failure, social, political and economic change, employment   turnover,   population   increase   and   technological breakthrough such as we have never experienced before. We are in a time of rapid, ceaseless and chaotic change. We can no longer count   on   having   stable   relationships,   stable   conditions   of employment or stable social patterns. It's not a matter of learning the game and playing it well. We now have to constantly learn new games, many of which are half conceived with changeable rules or no rules at all.

Dealing with changes

We have been poorly socialised to deal with this change. Firstly, we are still looking outside ourselves for the answers. We are still looking for someone who knows how things should be, how we should act and what the right outcome should be. The more rapid the change, the fewer the people that really know and understand what is happening. Despite this, we all spend a huge amount of time looking for concrete evidence and authoritative people to tell us the answers. Our socialisation has been so successful that few of us will risk taking a stand based on our own experience of reality, what we believe to be right and our own sense of personal responsibility.

Secondly, for individuals to cope successfully with change they need to be able to fully experience and accept their emotional response to the change. For most of us our socialisation involved a process of learning to discredit our own emotional response if it was different or unacceptable to our caregivers, that is, to experience reality as a function of what was acceptable to other, and deny (repress) any emotions that appeared to be at odds with the expectations of those we valued.

As an organisational change agent I constantly experience the terror that rises in people when they are faced with change. Change removes our old signposts, makes it clear that we no longer know which way to go, who to follow or whose approval and support we need to gain. I learnt a long time ago, however, that if I ask people about these fears the majority will deny they are experiencing any fear at all. Initially I thought that people didn't want to admit publicly to what they perceived as a weakness. It took me some time to realise that most people were so emotionally numb they actually didn't realise that they were frightened. Ironically, they were able to witness and understand the fear in others while denying the same discomfort in themselves.

William Webster revisited

For leaders like William Webster rapid change poses some real problems. Firstly, William got to be successful by working out what others wanted and giving it to them. He learnt this at home where his father, a successful businessman, and his mother, a noted socialite, rewarded him richly for conformity to their standards of hard work, social etiquette and maintenance of public appearance. At school he learnt that these same values lead to acclaim and popularity, which were reinforced by the approval of his parents. Once in the world of work, William knew well how to ascertain his employer's needs and meet them. He quickly rose to the top.

He'd been schooled from birth to lead. What William didn't know was how to change. His way of being in the world was so solid and fixed and had been so heavily reinforced that William had difficulty in letting go of what he knew and moving through unknown territory to new ways. Moreover, because his way of being was so socially acceptable he had difficulty seeing that the set of beliefs, skills and personal characteristics that had lead to his success were the same beliefs, skills and characteristics that were now causing him problems.

William's single-minded focus on his objectives had lead to achieving his goals. This same focus had stopped him from being present and available for relationships. William's ability to suss out the needs of his superiors had led to his rapid rise to the top but had also robbed him of his ability to experience and handle his own needs with respect. His ability to fit in and to be socially acceptable had denied him the opportunity to experience his own emotions and inner guidance or to follow his own lead. William was locked tightly in the box of his own success. It was when this success was thwarted that he began to look for the key that would unlock him.

Peaceful Chaos

Peaceful Chaos is the art of leadership in times of rapid change. It is the way of putting back into your life the elements of you that socialisation has had you give up.

Peaceful Chaos is not the only path to success. It is a path to success that will work for you in times of rapid change in a way that will enrich your quality of life at home and at work. The aim of Peaceful Chaos is to lead in a way that enhances:

- your sense of self
- enjoyment in your work
- the quality of your relationships
- your peace of mind
- your openness to growth and change

In times of rapid change:

those with a strong sense of self will have the emotional stability to successfully cope with their own change and the change of those they lead;

those with enjoyment in their work will have the humour, motivation and staying power to ride with the storms and be replenished in the lulls;

those with high quality relationships will have the emotional and physical support to achieve their goals, replenish their souls and enjoy their work, rest and play;

those with peace of mind will have the ability to cope with stress, think clearly, see through the debris to the real issues, maintain their vision and composure and learn from and fully experience the richness of their life as it changes;

those with openness to growth and learning will have the ability to adapt to situations in a way that enhances their belief in themselves, enhances their ability to lead and enhances their personal and professional well–being and success.

As with William, the road to Peaceful Chaos is often undertaken when our own success is blocked by a change in our circumstances. It makes sense that we will go on operating the way we know until that way proves not to work.

My path to Peaceful Chaos

When I graduated from business school I was, I thought, well equipped to operate in the business world. I had an impressive academic record as well as years of experience as a Chief Executive Officer and as an academic. I had spent time working for a prestigious institute researching trends in management. I was loaded with the tools and experience to become successful in my chosen field of consulting to management in the area of organisational change and I had a proven track record in a variety of leadership positions. I was young, attractive, ambitious and clear-sighted, or so it appeared to me at the time.

Others seemed to agree with me and I quickly became successful, helping senior managers of large organisations prepare corporate strategies, restructure their organisations, deal with takeovers and mergers and a variety of other major changes. Despite my success, something inside me said that there had to be more.

I watched people engage in the art of organisational politics, undermining each other, denying the truth, playing games and working themselves into self-induced illness. I noticed the poverty of their relationships, the lack of quality work-life and the pressure that senior managers put on their families. I saw executives engage in 'stress management' programs, race off to 'time management' courses and pursue a constant search for better and easier ways of winning in a highly competitive, people-consuming world.

The effect of all this on their staff was dramatic. Most people in the organisations I visited worked in fear. They constantly had their antennae alert for the whim of their superiors so that they could act in the most politically sensitive way. This had more to do with a desire to survive than any cynical attempt at coercion. Organisations were, it seemed to me, pretty inhuman places, places where people's feelings, needs and well-being were totally subservient to reaching objectives. Further, it appeared that failing to take into account people's feelings, needs and well-being was a guaranteed way of limiting productivity and goal attainment.

Why, I wondered, couldn't people be more honest and supportive with each other? Why couldn't they behave at work more like they did at home?

Then I realised that in fact they *were* behaving at work in a very similar manner to the way they behaved at home. I looked at the statistics on family violence, emotional abuse, alcoholism, drug addiction, work addiction, psychological illness and family breakdown and realised that people at work were behaving the only way they knew how. Most people, it appeared, didn't know how to relate to others in ways that were nurturing, supportive and conducive to productive living. What was worse was that the problem was so widespread everybody thought that the gross inhumanity that people displayed to each other was normal; it was all they had ever known. Nobody seemed to like the situation very much but people generally agreed that this was the way things had always been and would always be; there was simply no alternative.

A quick search of management literature confirmed that management theory and practice had very little to offer in terms of finding a more human, honest and reality-based way of doing business. Even authors who purport to bring a new approach, for example, many New Age writers, seemed to be doing little more than using new and more sophisticated psychological techniques to perpetuate the status quo.

Around this time a series of blessings came my way disguised as disasters. My first marriage failed. Then my daughter contracted a life-threatening disease and nearly died. My father began a cancer-induced decline towards death. I entered into a rather unwise business partnership. To compound all this, I placed myself in a series of destructive, if short-lived, relationships.

Eventually things got so bad I was forced to admit that I was nowhere near as together, in control or perfect as I had thought. What was perhaps even more disturbing was the realisation that my fascination with other people's problems was a direct result of my unwillingness to deal with my own and to get down to the hard work of facing and working through my own illusions. As I began to do this I made the further rather uncomfortable discovery that my drive for success was at least in part due to my desire to keep too busy to face up to the reality that was my life. I had created for myself a socially accepted, and in fact acclaimed, mechanism for keeping myself neurotic. I was too successful to notice that my life had been based on very rocky foundations.

I began to increase my self–awareness, to surface and come to terms with what drove me and to recall the childhood experiences behind these drives. I learnt to live comfortably with my emotions and began to let down the egoic defences that I had so cleverly erected to keep me safe and which I later learnt were responsible for most of my unhappiness and feelings of alienation.

This meant giving up the need to plan for every eventuality, to control every situation and to continuously organise myself and others. It meant learning to feel and express my emotions, to come to terms with my own weaknesses and vulnerability and to adapt to new ways of relating.

I found this journey very difficult. I was very unskilled at finding safe people, and continually surrounded myself with people who attacked my feeble attempts to change. These people proved to be a blessing in the long run because I learnt how to grow in a hostile environment.

From private life to public success

Initially I separated my own growth from the work I did, but as time passed it became harder and harder for me to keep myself out of my work. I was therefore faced with the dilemma of merging what seemed to be two totally opposed worlds—the highly competitive world of business and public life with the haven of safety I was beginning to create in my own life. I felt as though I was walking on the edge of two facing cliffs.   My fear was that I seemed to continually fall between the cracks, into the precipice in the middle.

What I learnt at business school seemed to make less and less sense, and what I was learning in my own life seemed to be all that mattered. How, I wondered, was I going to make a living and support my family? Slowly, very slowly, I began to bring more of myself to my work. I began to talk with my clients about my experiences with my children, about my own growth and about the issues that faced me in my life at that moment. I started to share with my clients the world that I was beginning to enjoy so much—my world.

I also shared with them the exercises that I had devised or adapted to help me in my life. I felt nervous doing this because I was way out of my territory. I'd spent 10 years as an academic, where everything was researched, debated and supported. I had no proof that what we were doing would work, yet in my heart I knew that the old ways just didn't make sense and that maybe together my clients and I could find a new way.

My courage seemed to pay off. Instead of going from short assignment to short assignment, my clients started to engage me for longer periods. It seemed that the techniques and ways of relating that we were learning together were providing them with big benefits. They were more rested, happier, clearer in their thinking, more creative and found that they and their organisations were able to change much more readily and with less strain all around. Like me, my clients had great difficulty explaining to anyone what we were doing or why it worked, but the results were unmistakable. Like me, they learnt not to preach or try to convert others but simply to share their personal insights with anyone who made inquiries. They learnt to let people see for themselves what the benefits might be.

In the meantime my income increased and the demand for my services began to outstrip the supply. It was time to look at finding ways to teach others to do my work so that the demand could be filled.

The problem was that I didn't know what I did. Sure, there were some ideas and some exercises, but I knew this wasn't what worked. I was well aware that another person could espouse those same ideas and teach those same exercises and no real change would occur. What worked was the process, the dynamics that happened between my clients and me, and that had nothing to do with the content of what was said or what was done.

What worked was my ability to isolate as role models a number of personal attributes and attitudes that are currently not even recognised as valuable in public life. These included the ability to 'not know', a willingness to 'unlearn' and the courage to be 'real'. Time and time again I found myself in front of groups of high–flying executives realising that I had not a clue what I was doing, not because I was incompetent but because what we were doing we had never done before. I didn't know because it was unknowable. At such times I would feel a rush of fear shoot up my spine. How could I take such risks? Then I realised that most of us don't know most of the time, we just don't admit it to ourselves and others. We surround ourselves with delusions of knowing and pretend that they are real. We follow formulae, tested methods and familiar paths because we think that this way we will know, but all we know is how to fool ourselves. Every time we apply a formula or method in a new situation we are in a place of unknowing. We don't know what the outcome will be and if we were honest we don't know the implications of what we are doing. Not knowing is common, admitting it is rare.

Once I was able to face the fact that I generally didn't know, I was able to start giving up all the techniques, games, tricks, defences and delusions that I had acquired to assist the pretence that

I was in control. It seemed I had spent a lifetime acquiring a whole lot of intellectual and emotional baggage just in case I should ever find myself somewhere new and didn't know what to do. Rather than helping me be in control, this baggage stopped me from seeing life, people and myself as we were.

Letting go of control

The art of Peaceful Chaos is deceptively simple. It is merely to give up the illusion of control and the need to be perfect and accept yourself and reality exactly as they are. *That is it. There is no more to it than that.* It is encapsulated in the Sufi story of the man who was swimming up river with his clothes on looking for a way of making his journey easier.

Peaceful Chaos would simply suggest that it takes super-human amounts of energy to do impossible things and it often makes a lot more sense to stop doing what you are doing, review your actions to date, review your motivation and make some new choices, like taking your clothes off, swimming with the current not against it, or deciding you'll get further if you walk. Nothing revolutionary about that, except that people will fight tooth and nail not to do it. We are such creatures of habit that if we are used to swimming against the current fully clad we are likely to believe that this is the best if not the only way to go about things, it's the way it has always been done. We will look at the people swimming freely downstream and comment on their lack of effort as if it were a fault, some flaw in their character that they chose the easier path. We will look at the scantily clad swimmer and comment on his lack of morality and at the walker and comment on his abuse of the environment or folly for working up a sweat. We will invest huge amounts of time and energy looking for someone who will tell us how to swim up-stream fully clad, more efficiently, rather than stop and face our own truth that perhaps we are asking the wrong questions.

Leadership under question

We continue a social masquerade that some people, who we call leaders, have the answers and will be able to show us how to cope and how to solve our problems. Even those of us who call ourselves leaders look for people on whom to shift the responsibility for our decisions. We look for expert advisers, government assistance and union cooperation to underwrite our success and carry the blame for our losses.

As a society we are prepared to pay leaders handsomely. We will pay well for their books, their advice and their patronage. We watch them on television, listen to them on the radio, attend their conferences and buy their tapes and videos. We go to their seminars, complete their workbooks and wait patiently for their insights. Some of us even follow them around the world and worship at their feet. We so much want someone to show us, to lead us, to teach us and to help us get it right.

There are many people around who are happy to oblige our need for directive leadership. Many people holding positions of power have the misguided belief that being a leader means telling others what to do and how to do it. Unconsciously, they convince themselves, that leaders need to be slightly Godlike. Leaders, they believe need to know what is going to happen and prepare their followers to capitalise on the future or avert its misfortunes. There is a strong myth that leaders can predict the future, plan for the contingencies, organise and control people to fit the plan and keep themselves in constant command. In fact these are the basic tenets of conventional management and are taught as such in most management courses around the world.

Well, Chaos Theory tells us that nobody can know what is going to happen because it is unknowable, and that attempts to force reality to be a certain way are likely to bring about more unpredictable change than we are trying to avert. Our own common sense tells us that anyone who thinks they can see into the future and control the elements of a living system has to be suffering from delusions of grandeur and is therefore untrustworthy.

Leaders who try to be all things to all people, who try to emulate God, simply create dependency in their followers. There are enough people around who want to be told what to do and who want to believe that there are universal answers to ensure that anyone posing as a font of all wisdom will attract a following. That following is looking for an excuse not to lead their own lives and not to find their own answers; in short, they are looking for a scapegoat and an excuse not to learn and grow. In stable times such games are foolish: in times of rapid change they are suicidal.

Towards a new definition of leadership

With the old standards of leadership being of decreasing use to leaders and followers alike, it is time to find a new way to lead, a way that allows us to deal with change, face reality and improve the quality of our work and private lives.

Such a model was provided for me by the managers of a prestigious bank. I asked these executives to draw me a caricature of a 'real' leader, one who was a composite of leaders they had experienced personally, leaders to whom they felt loyal and who had inspired them to be, do and achieve more.

The picture that emerged was one of 'a human being who leads'. The figure was

androgynous because leaders can be of either sex;

had large eyes because leaders are visionary and clear-sighted;

had a large, open mouth because leaders are skilled communicators;

had big ears because leaders are good listeners;

had broad shoulders because leaders take responsibility;

had strong hands because leaders can handle every situation;

had a babe in arms because leaders are caring;

had pants on because leaders are modest;

had strong legs because leaders stand their ground;

had one leg in front of the other because leaders move forward;

had one leg stationary because leaders are stable and a point of reference;

had big feet because leaders are 'down to earth';

walked on a path because leaders know where they are going.

'Leaders', the bankers told me, are very human people. They are like all of us only more so.

This definition fits well with me. It says that we are all leaders. To varying degrees we are all visionary, strong, caring, responsible and clear–sighted. We are all listeners, communicators and trendsetters. We are all human. The people who stand out ahead of the others are those who choose to be more human than the rest of us.

We are all born leaders. No one is more human than a baby. Babies feel free to be totally human. Then comes socialisation, and we very quickly learn to follow, to conform to the dictates of our parents, our siblings, our teachers and our peers. We eventually reach a stage where we have lost touch with the very humanity we need in order to make full use of our lives. We search around for someone else to tell us how we should live, what decisions we should make, what clothes we should wear, where we should live and how we should raise our children.   We look to others for information, suggestions and answers and then we blame them when things don't turn out the way we think they should. We end up living our lives to a script that we have asked our parents, partners, employers, politicians, the media and many others to write for us.

Having exchanged our independence for social acceptance, we try desperately to control whatever remains within our realm. We search out situations and relationships that reinforce our world view and do whatever we can to avoid or manipulate people and events which challenge our illusions about the way things are. By restricting and controlling our environment we reinforce our view that life can be predictable, planned, pleasant and easy—if only we can do the right things and find the right answers.

Leading our own way

If 'leaders are very human people', then leadership is about experiencing and coming to terms with our humanity. We are all walking a path that has never been travelled before and will never be travelled again. Each person's journey is unique. We are the only one who can truly know how it is for us to face the huge array of changing situations that arise in our lifetime. Only we can decide what we want to achieve, how we want to live our lives and what matters for us. Only we can decide whether to enjoy this lifetime or to spend it in isolation and misery. We are our own leaders.

Some people, however, are so good at leading their own lives that other people want to learn from them. They say, 'Hey, fellow traveller, you seem to be getting more fun, success, peace and joy out of all this than the rest of us. Can we journey beside you for a while? Can we look into your world and see how it works for you? We might learn something.' The leader, pleased to have the company and an opportunity to gain the insights of another, agrees and for a time leader and follower align their journeys and travel on parallel tracks.

Out of this the leader learns and grows, and for a time feels less lonely, less separate and less different. The follower learns how it is for another, someone who may be a little further down the track. The follower then applies this learning to their own life and increases their own sense of leadership.

Inherent in all this is a wonderful liberation. If we are the only ones who can 'lead' our lives for us, if life is about constant, ceaseless, unpredictable change, if leadership is about being human, then all we have to do to be a leader, to find our own answers and live our lives in richness and peace, is to stop fighting reality and accept ourselves as human beings. The more fully we do this, the more likely we are to succeed and to be the kind of person others will follow. Moreover, leadership from this perspective becomes not a burden or a responsibility but a blessing. It offers us the joy of sharing our insights, lives and energy with others, thus reducing the stress and the loneliness that we all feel as we tread our this–life journey.

So being a leader isn't about telling others what to do, organising others, controlling the present or the future or trying to create things to be the way we think they should be. Leadership is about living our life in fullness, peace and good health and by so doing setting others an example that they may wish to follow.

Chapter 2

Finding The Essence

Mary is a merchant banker. She's bright, ambitious and on the way up. Mary is married to Ted. They have a five–year–old daughter Fiona, an old English sheep dog called Nelson and a full–time, live–in housekeeper–nanny. Mary is in line to become a director of her firm, a post she will probably achieve within the next 18 months. What is it like to be Mary on an average day?

Mary gets up about 5.30 a.m. and goes for a jog—she thinks it's important for her to keep fit so that she can manage the pressure of her job. She also sees her appearance as part of her competitive advantage. After her run Mary has her shower, washes her hair, puts on her make-up, dresses and blow–dries her hair before Fiona wakes up and they have breakfast together. Then Mary's in the car and at the office by 8.00 a.m.

Today is just a normal day. She sees a range of clients, finalises a strategic planning submission to the Board, and talks with her staff about their work. Her secretary Martha is having problems coping at the moment—her husband left her 2 years ago and as a single parent she's finding it difficult to manage everything. Mary thinks how lucky she is to be able to afford live–in help.

Today Mary is lunching with a reporter from a women's magazine which is running a story on high–flying women. Mary enjoys the opportunity to share with other women what she has achieved; she hopes that it will inspire them to widen their horizons.

After lunch Mary remembers that she's promised to watch Fiona sing in the concert her kindergarten is performing for Senior Citizens' week.   Mary worries that Fiona doesn't see her much. Mary fails to turn up to so many school events—so often just as she is running out the door, the managing director or some major client wants to see her.

However, this time Mary makes the concert. She hopes Fiona can see her in the audience as she sits there looking interested but actually worrying about the client meeting she has at 4.30 p.m. Mary mutters to herself, 'These school concerts are so badly organised, they always have the children performing for far too long. Still Fiona does seem to be enjoying herself.'

Back at the office Mary returns 10 of the 15 calls that came in while she was out. She prepares for her client meeting and liaises with a colleague to ensure that she has all the information that she needs. The client meeting goes well, so well in fact that the client invites her out for drinks. She ensures that one of her colleagues joins them—this looks more businesslike. Mary arrives home at 7.30 p.m. Dinner is ready, as usual. She talks with Ted and Fiona about their day before putting Fiona to bed at 8.30 p.m. and reading her a story. Mary then falls into a chair in front of the TV. She watches the pre-taped international news before skimming the financial press. Exhausted, she's in bed by 9.30 p.m. She kisses Ted goodnight and as she falls asleep remembers that it is some time since she and Ted made love—pity, she does enjoy it when she has the time and energy.

Mary has everything. She has an understanding husband, a beautiful daughter, a successful career, plenty of money and a full-time person to keep her house functioning smoothly. Mary looks great, sounds great and is definitely on her way to the top. Her day is run in a way that ensures that everything gets done. She is very reliable, very efficient, very considerate and very dead. Mary lives her life like clockwork, ticking off the hours and days as items on her busy agenda. She frets that she doesn't spend enough time with her child, her husband, her friends or her extended family. She feels that she is letting the family team down. She worries that her family responsibilities interfere with her full participation at work, but she isn't going to let being a woman get in the way of her career. She harbours a secret desire that one day she will have time to paint and revive her skill on the piano, but she just has too many people relying on her at the moment. Mary has time for everything but living.

Peaceful Chaos and change

There's an old Buddhist saying which says:

> Before enlightenment—chop wood, carry water;
> after enlightenment—chop wood, carry water.

Peaceful Chaos leadership is not so much about the way you act as it is about the way you feel. It is a very private transformation.

In the West we have usually demanded that change be visible and result in a measurable difference. In management, the 'science' of measuring things that are intangible has reached ridiculous proportions. It's as though we believe that if something isn't measurable it isn't worth anything. My experience is that many of the changes we witness aren't changes at all, they are just the same old thing dished up in a measurably different way. The process of Peaceful Chaos is a process wherein nothing may appear to be different and yet nothing will ever be the same again.

I have a philosophy that the best way to change any organisation is to work over a period of time helping the people who lead that organisation to move into Peaceful Chaos.   Most of my clients approach me because they have heard of my success in organisational change and want me to change the people who work for them. They complain that many of these people are resistant to change. Time and again we find that as the leaders move into Peaceful Chaos their staff, even those previously antagonistic to new ways, start asking if they can join the leaders change process. They have noticed their leaders relaxing, having greater clarity of vision, being more approachable, more human, happier and more content. Seeing real change in their leaders and experiencing the benefits of these changes they are sold on change for themselves.

This is very different to the usual practice of leaders preaching change but not engaging in any themselves. Though most leaders have difficulty delegating, I have noticed that they rarely hesitate to delegate growth and change, thus reinforcing the idea that powerful people do not have to develop—they have already made it. Change by rhetoric and abdication doesn't work because people see with their own eyes that growth and change are lower status activities.

In today's environment this is the death knell. With so much instability in every area of public and private life it is only those who can grow and change who will come out on top. Those who are the model for growth and learning are today's effective leaders.

Managers are people too

For many years I have felt exhausted after reading books like *In Search Of Excellence, Thriving on Chaos* and *Iacocca: An Autobiography* because they seemed to be full of things that I should do, things that didn't seem to have anything to do with being human or, more particularly, with being me. It seemed that I was being told that success in public life involved playing a range of complex, competitive games. Management books, courses and gurus seemed to be telling me that success rested on learning the best moves and playing them in order to win. The message seemed to be that winning was more important than achieving in a way that enhanced my sense of self and vitality. It seemed that I was being encouraged to have a public self at the expense of my emotional, spiritual and physical well–being.

My explorations into the fields of psychotherapy, family therapy and the recovery movement showed me that there was another way to run my public life, a way that enhanced both my private and public success.

The model on the following page helps me explain how we can begin to move from old–style leadership into Peaceful Chaos.

We all have within us three layers of experience and reality.
These are

ESSENTIAL YOU

WOUNDED YOU

DEFENDED YOU

At our core is **ESSENTIAL YOU**. This is our genetic inheritance.

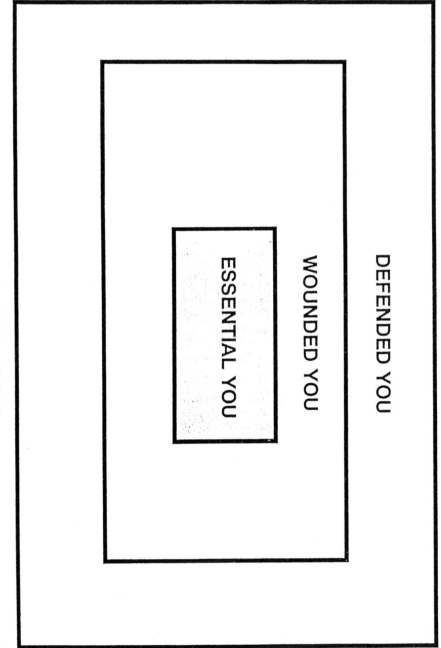

DEFENDED YOU

WOUNDED YOU

ESSENTIAL YOU

ESSENTIAL YOU contains our potential to:

> feel • be real • play • have fun and be childlike • have a rich spiritual life • be clear and direct • be powerful in the true sense • be expansive and loving • be communicative and giving • be open to growth and learning • enjoy ourselves as sensual beings • accept ourselves and others • dream and hold a vision • develop our unique gifts, talents and perspectives • find, hold and follow a true sense of purpose • be open to our unconscious • have a rich private, inner life • be creative • be intuitive • be human • be genuine • be spontaneous • be vulnerable • be compassionate • be assertive • think clearly.

WOUNDED YOU is our stunted 'child self', the part of ourselves that is ill-formed or repressed due to the process of socialisation. WOUNDED YOU holds within it unresolved emotional trauma and the foggy thinking of the 'old brain'.
WOUNDED YOU contains

> repressed childhood hurts • self-judgement • denied parts of our essential selves • self-limiting beliefs

DEFENDED YOU is the set of defences we have built up to protect WOUNDED YOU and keep the world at bay. DEFENDED YOU is the face we most often show the world. It is the mask behind which we hide to keep ourselves safe.
DEFENDED YOU contains our defences of

> dumping our anger on others • being a nice boy/girl • pleasing others • rejecting others • intimidating others •

playing the victim ● taking responsibility for others ● failing to listen to others ● judging self/others ● failing to listen to ourselves ● alcoholism ● overeating ● aggressiveness and/or passivity ● pretence of strength at all times ● pretence of always knowing ● avoidance of being nurtured by others ● overreliance on rationality ● dependence on external power bases ● blocking unconscious material ● hiding behind a false persona ● obsessive control ● winning at all costs ● living in our heads ● denying our emotions ● throwing tantrums ● being indispensable ● withdrawing love ● failing to listen to self/others ● violence ● self–induced illness ● drug dependence ● self–righteousness ● denying reality.

ESSENTIAL YOU

When each of us is born we are 100 per cent ESSENTIAL YOU.

ESSENTIAL YOU is our genetic inheritance. It is what makes us human. It is our ability to feel, to think, to create and to be uniquely ourselves. Each of us is born with immense potential, some of which we hold in common with all human beings and some of which is distinctively ours. For babies it's all the same. They just revel in the sensuous delight of being alive. They place no judgement on whether what they do or how they feel is right or wrong. They just do and feel! From this wonderful self–acceptance they have a hunger for learning and for life.

Within our ESSENTIAL YOU lies all the potential we need to have full, enjoyable and creative lives. Our ESSENTIAL YOU is our personal leadership resource kit. Unfortunately most of us have lost full access to it.

WOUNDED YOU

As babies we depend on the adults in our lives for our very survival. Although as babies we are totally accepting of ourselves and others, the adults on whom we depend have difficulty completely embracing our untamed humanity. They let us know that some parts of our Essential Selves aren't acceptable. They do this through a system of rewards and punishments, some of which are overt and some of which come in the form of a frown, the withdrawal of love or a non–verbal threat. Some of this socialisation makes sense and some of it is the result of ignorance or habit on the part of our parents or caregivers.

The process of socialisation is imperfect. Unfortunately no one knows how to rear babies in a way that allows them to become successfully socialised without losing some of their Essential Selves.

It might seem like a truism but babies think like babies and adults think like adults. For a baby, having their natural toilet, eating and crying impulses restricted, modified and not accepted, can easily be taken as a personal rejection of them. As they develop, infants learn to fit in to the routine of their homes by rejecting whatever parts of their Essential Selves appear to be unacceptable to their caregivers. This may be the baby's tendency to pull out mother's hair or bite the cat, but often it also includes the baby's boundless energy and curiosity, which parents find exhausting or dangerous. If parents have trouble accepting emotional expression or sexual exploration these also become off–limits and repressed.

There is no fault on anyone's part in this. It's not that parents are good or bad, although some parents are undoubtedly more loving and accepting than others. It is just that adults operate out of their imperatives, barely realising the effect these have on infants, who see the world from the perspective of someone who is vulnerable, dependant, inexperienced and whose thinking processes are immature. The outcome of this is that we learn at an early age to judge ourselves, develop negative beliefs about our worth and ability and we push from our consciousness those parts of ourselves we perceive to be unacceptable to adults.

Although from an adult viewpoint modifying the behaviour of an infant makes sense, for the growing child it is extremely painful to have personal characteristics, part of the ESSENTIAL YOU, rejected by parents and others. As children we are too vulnerable and dependent to deal with the full impact of socialisation. Children so desperately need love that failure to receive contact, warmth and love can actually lead to 'failure to thrive' and death.   When babies are denied approval (love) for being themselves, the terror and hurt is therefore the fear of death. This fear is overwhelming and is quickly repressed into the 'old brain'.

The 'old brain'

Harville Hendrix in his book *Getting the Love You Want* explains that we have two physically identifiable parts to our brain. The 'old brain' and the 'new brain' The **new brain** is the part which we know. It 'makes decisions, thinks, observes, plans, anticipates, responds, organises information and creates ideas'. The **old brain**, however, is only interested in 'self–preservation'. Through a series of fuzzy images that have no sense of linear time, our old brain is preoccupied with primal issues such as nurturing, being nurtured, sex, escape, submission, attack, out of our conscious awareness, and based on primal questions of safety and reproduction, our old brain is the part of us that drives many of our basic decisions, actions thoughts and emotions.

Unlike the 'new brain' which we know and trust, our 'old brain' is neither rational nor logical. It makes its decisions based on memories that are forgotten to our conscious mind and which the 'old brain' carries around as being current, as if they were happening now. For example, if when you were young you had an aunt who hurt you, and as an adult you see a person who has the same 'feel' to you as the aunt, you will have exactly the same response as an adult that you had as a baby. The response will have the same intense impact over your actions as when you were young. The problem is, you are unlikely to be conscious of how you feel or how your response drives your actions. The 'old brain' represents a whole system of thought and feeling that is as applicable and rational for making adult decisions as the mind of a young child. The only interest this part of our brain has is to keep us safe, safety being defined by the needs and wants of an infant.

As if this isn't confusing enough, modern psychological research tells us that most of us are suffering from unhealed childhood wounds that impede our ability to mature and develop as rational, fully functioning adults. These wounds are a direct result of being a child growing up in a twentieth century nuclear family. No matter how well intentioned our parents were they were unable to meet our endless needs for emotional, spiritual and physical support, love and approval. The result is that most of us reach adulthood having recognised but a small amount of our Essential Selves while harbouring within us a mass of self-defeating beliefs, repressed emotions and self doubts, most of which are hidden out of our conscious awareness in our 'old brains'.

For years I have stood next to executives who have behaved for all the world like two-year-olds. They have insisted there were no problems when there obviously were, they have thrown tantrums and called each other names. They have avoided the facts and denied the undeniable. It was a great liberation for me to discover that this was a result of a real and identifiable phenomena, the 'old brain'.

Under every apparently upstanding, intelligent, successful leader is a little boy or girl—a WOUNDED YOU—full of self-doubt, fear and pain.

The nature of the 'old brain' is such that we will fight to defend our WOUNDED YOU as if our lives depend on it. For the 'old brain' life and death is all there is and rejection of the ESSENTIAL YOU is tantamount to death.

DEFENDED YOU

We suppressed the painful emotions of our socialisation into our 'old brain' early, we then built up a system of defences to ensure that we never had to feel those painful emotions again. Every person has their own set of defences; they differ but we all have them. It is our way of structuring our world so that we can operate without full access to our ESSENTIAL YOU and without feeling the pain of WOUNDED YOU. Our defences, governed by our 'old brain', act to protect us from further hurt and help us avoid feeling the wounds that have already been inflicted.

In our society a common defence is to maintain an outward focus on the world. This focus has us place our attention on what we can see and measure rather than how we feel. By constantly focusing on other people, on the environment or on the problem, we are provided with a socially sanctioned defence that allows us to avoid noticing how we feel. This defence also denies us the ability to fully enjoy our lives and to relate successfully to others. As most people are operating out of the same defence, we accept our behaviour as normal.

Mary revisited

Let's return to Mary. She never thinks about herself, her whole focus is on Fiona, Ted, the clients, her staff, her colleagues, other women and the housekeeper (whose name she continually forgets). Mary is always helping these people to understand, to learn, to grow, to achieve more and to be more powerful. Mary wants to see other people have all the things that she has. She wants them to do well and to succeed. By helping them she feels needed, useful, purposeful and in control. She knows that people appreciate her and that this allows her to continue to be successful herself. She calls this her win-win style of management.

But is it? Another way of looking at it might be that by focusing all her attention on others Mary fails to notice the hollowness of her life. She goes through the motions of being human. She has a daughter she hardly sees, who has been trained to fit in, be convenient and make Mummy's busy life easier. She has a husband with whom she swaps pleasantries and occasional bouts of sexual activity. She lives with a housekeeper she doesn't know. Her relationships with her staff are paternalistic and manipulative. Her colleagues appreciate her thoughtfulness but know that they have to keep her on-side because of her growing network and power base. Her clients appreciate the fact that their affairs are competently and capably handled. Her employers like the fact that Mary makes them money, doesn't cause them problems and is pleasant to have around, not to mention good to look at.

Who really cares about Mary—about how she feels, about her fears, sensitivities, feelings of inadequacy and self-doubts? Who knows about her need to be loved and accepted just for herself, without having to perform, look good or achieve? The answer is nobody, not even Mary.

Mary learnt early that only 'good little girls' were rewarded with love and attention. 'Naughty girls' were sent to their room or emotionally shut out. Mary grew up as a people pleaser. By focusing on doing the right things and staying in control, Mary was able to avoid feeling the pain of rejection and maintain the illusion that she could be loved and looked after only if she did the right things and made everybody happy. The only person who wasn't happy was Mary. She was hassled, full of self–doubts and fears and terrified that if she messed up in any area of her life she would be alone and unloved. She managed to keep herself sufficiently busy so as not to feel, because she didn't like what happened when she did. Along with the self–doubts and fears, Mary's decision to not feel denied her the ability to experience love, contentment, joy and peace.

Mary's 'good girl' defences had worked to make her very successful and avoided her experiencing a lot of 'old brain' wounds. It had also served to deny her full access to her ESSENTIAL YOU.

Retrieving the ESSENTIAL YOU

As I have said, we start off as pure ESSENTIAL YOU. We then deny parts of our essence in order to please those on whom we as children depend. This denial causes us pain that we find too overwhelming and therefore repress into our 'old brain'. These denied parts of ourselves keep us from reclaiming ESSENTIAL YOU. To avoid the pain of feeling our WOUNDED YOU and from being distant from our ESSENTIAL YOU we build up defences that become our chief way of operating in the world. In time we actually begin to think we are our defences.

Public life as I have experienced it is lived almost entirely on the level of DEFENDED YOU. People relate, behave and think not from the clarity and heart of ESSENTIAL YOU but from the defended position from which they feel safe. I'm not saying that our defences don't have a place, they definitely do, it is just that they have often become our entire repertoire. We don't know how to do anything but defend. I can't, for instance, remember reading one management, public speaking or negotiation book that didn't operate on the level of improving the operation of the defences. From memory, my entire MBA degree was a course in how to be better defended.

Defences help to keep us from hurting, they also stop us relating, blind us to reality and keep us separate from our ESSENTIAL YOU wherein lies our prime source of energy, creativity, joy, peace, natural talent and personal well-being. Because the majority of people in public life are operating out of their DEFENDED YOU we assume that this is the norm. However the norm is so much less than what is possible and serves to separate public success from personal well-being.

It doesn't have to be this way

Lying within our ESSENTIAL YOU is all the potential we need to be successful in our public and private lives. There is all the strength, insight, drive, talent and love that will ensure that we can succeed in a way that is in harmony with our own being. It makes sense that those who succeed by being in harmony with themselves are in a position to go further and sustain their success longer than those who have to fight and suppress their natural energy to achieve.

The problem is that access to our ESSENTIAL YOU is blocked firstly by our WOUNDED YOU and secondly by our DEFENDED YOU. If we shift the defences, we feel the pain of

WOUNDED YOU as well as the joy of ESSENTIAL YOU. For most of us the experience of the pain overshadows the delight of ESSENTIAL YOU and we quickly replace our defences.   This is particularly so if we let down our defences in a public arena where we are often met by others' DEFENDED YOU and feel attacked and wounded further. Anyone who has experienced this is unlikely to be in a hurry to repeat the experience. This way we keep each other in our defences, nothing changes and nobody grows. The status quo is maintained.

The work I do assists people to slowly improve their access to their ESSENTIAL YOU. Working with top organisational teams I help leaders realise the following things.

1   DEFENDED YOU serves a purpose.

You developed your DEFENDED YOU because you needed it. It helped protect you from pain that was previously intolerable. It still helps to protect you from those people whose defences you find painful. It makes absolutely no sense to take down your defences to be wounded all over again. Your DEFENDED YOU got you this far, now you need to

- get to know it
- accept it
- respect it

Many of the defences that you developed early in life have become so ingrained you don't even know you have them. Moreover, while many of them have a real function, your level of unconsciousness around your defences is likely to be so great that you will defend as a matter of course whether it is appropriate or not. It's a bit like always going out wearing a raincoat because you once got wet. By getting to know, accept and respect your defences you can notice when they work for you and when they don't. It allows you to shift information from your 'old brain' to your 'new brain' and places you more in control of your life and your actions. So when it rains you can wear your raincoat when it doesn't you can leave it in the closet.

Getting to know your defences allows you to realise what you are doing and decide whether or not it works for you. Accepting your defences allows you to make choices about your behaviour by keeping your defences as part of your repertoire—you don't have to throw the raincoat out because you sometimes wear it unnecessarily. Respecting your defences allows them to become your friends rather than your enemies; this both raises your self-acceptance and gives you more choice as to your future patterns of thought, feeling and action.

The more at home you become with DEFENDED YOU, the less defended you will need to be. You are likely to start choosing to defend only when you need to rather than as a matter of course.

2   The pain is inside you.

One of the things that encourages us to remain defended is that when we let the defences down we feel pain. We rationalise that this pain is the result of some outside influence against which we need to defend ourselves. If you think about it, however, the only place you can feel pain is within yourself. We all find different things painful and some of us feel more pain than others. It is very helpful when working our way through to ESSENTIAL YOU to realise that DEFENDED YOU was developed to stop us feeling pain.   Our pain is ours. We all have our own hot buttons, sore spots and Achilles heel. The secret is to know what yours are so that you can manage yourself and your behaviour.

The only person over whom any of us has any control is

ourself. We can do little to stop other people doing things that we find painful. We can, however, do a lot in response to our pain. We can move away from the source of pain, we can use the pain as a source of information from which to learn or we can simply feel the pain as a part of life.

Most of us are so frightened of pain that we defend against it constantly. In so doing we deaden all our emotions, distance ourselves from others and unconsciously deny a whole raft of useful information about ourselves, others and the world around us.

Pain itself isn't all that bad. What's wrong with feeling some pain from time to time? What causes us real problems isn't the pain, it's how we defend against the pain. Our defences have the potential to distort our thinking, our actions, our relationships and our credibility.

Once we realise that pain has many valuable lessons and uses we can begin to work with it to help us recover our ESSENTIAL YOU. Obviously the better use we make of our pain, the less defended we will need to be.

3   You need to build up ESSENTIAL YOU from within.

About five years into my own growth process I had moved a long way towards coming to terms with DEFENDED YOU and was increasingly comfortable with WOUNDED YOU when I hit a patch in my life where the pain became unbearable. I felt as though pain was everywhere and there was nowhere for me to escape. I was due to start a challenging major assignment and I had no idea how I was going to find the strength and courage to take a group of exacting executives through a demanding change process. Then the thought came to me that what I needed to do was *build myself up from the inside*. I needed some way of contacting my ESSENTIAL YOU and finding in it the vision, sustenance and strength that I needed.

At the same time I discovered in my bookshelf *Goodbye to Guilt*, a book written by psychiatrist Gerald Jampolski and based on *A Course in Miracles.* *Goodbye to Guilt* contained a series of exercises all of which involved contacting ESSENTIAL YOU and tapping into its strength. Throughout every day of that assignment I did those exercises. Every day I felt stronger, the pain became less and I felt increasingly at peace. I am now a regular student of *A Course in Miracles* and have made my spiritual practice a key part of my life. The assignment was a resounding success. One executive wrote: 'I have participated in one of the most profound experiences in both my work and personal life.'

I have noticed that after we have been working together for a while many of my clients return to their churches and religious practices. Those who are already practising a faith have told me that the process of moving towards Peaceful Chaos has helped them to more fully experience 'their God'.

Visualisation, meditation, prayer and quiet reflection all provide opportunities for contacting ESSENTIAL YOU. Unfortunately most busy leaders see time spent not doing anything as wasted time, rather than essential for enhancing their lifestyle and performance. We need emotional and spiritual sustenance as surely as we need food, drink, sleep and exercise.

4   Once you can do this for yourself, those around you will change without ever needing to know any of the theory or practice.

At the time I wrote this book, few of my clients had heard the terms ESSENTIAL YOU, WOUNDED YOU or DEFENDED YOU although all of them had experienced the benefits that stem from the model. For many of my clients the concepts inherent in this model would be threatening, yet they have all gained from my understanding and approach. When most people think about change they think about changing someone else.

I joke with my clients that no matter where I go in an organisation I am talking to the wrong person. The frontline person can't change because of the supervisor who can't change because of the manager who can't change because of the managing director who can't change because of the Board, the unions, the government and the financial markets. I call this the responsibility–free world in which nobody can change until everybody else does.

I have made my profession helping people bring about change. I learnt a long time ago that the best way to do that was to accept people as they are and concentrate on my own growth and learning. Using this approach I have achieved results that others claim to be impossible. It is only when people feel accepted and safe that they will take the risks inherent in letting down their defences, facing their pain and moving into ESSENTIAL YOU. All they need to start this process is motivation, support, love and a belief that it is possible. You can provide all that without ever saying a word—just by role modelling a different way.

People in most organisations complain that their leaders mouth one philosophy and live another. By role modelling change and creating around you an environment in which people feel safe enough to grow and learn, you can bring about infinitely greater changes than by repeating platitudes or forcing people to go to courses and meetings they really don't want to attend.

In many cases I am called in to work only on formulating a strategy or developing a marketing plan with senior management. At the end of such assignments people will often comment on a sense of peace, quiet and unity that forms in the management team. One management team with whom I had worked for some time claimed that they had become each other's best friends because they could talk more openly and honestly with each other than with friends outside work.   On one occasion I was amused when approached by a union leader who asked me to work with the management team of a major bank. I pointed out that for me to do that they needed to approach me, and inquired as to why he had contacted me. 'Well,' he said, 'you helped the managers of another bank put in their new strategy and my members said you turned the managers into human beings at the same time.'

Preaching, lecturing, forcing and pushing only causes resistance.   Leadership in times of change is all about showing people how to change by doing it yourself.

Contacting ESSENTIAL YOU

There are times in our lives when we are totally at peace with ourselves and the world around us.   They are magical moments when all is well with the world.   We feel strong, whole, connected with those around us and with our environment.   My clients relate that such times have occurred at the birth of their first child, when they saw their future wife walking down the aisle, when they completed a challenging assignment, walking on the beach, night fishing, making music with friends or love with their beloved. These are the times when we are in touch with our ESSENTIAL YOU.   Because contacting essential you is initially difficult, the following exercises have been designed to help you experience your own ESSENTIAL YOU.

After reading through the following exercise have someone you trust read it to you or tape it and play it back as you walk yourself through a guided visualisation where you revisit ESSENTIAL YOU. Experience once again what it is like to live in touch with your Essential Self.   The first part of the exercise is a relaxation exercise which I have found increases the openness of busy leaders to their ESSENTIAL YOU.

Relaxation exercise

Sit with your feet flat on the floor (remove high-heeled shoes), hands cupped in your lap and your eyes closed. Concentrate on your breath coming in and going out at its own pace.

Tense the muscles in your right foot, hold the tension for a few seconds, then relax the foot and let the tension run down through the sole of your foot into the ground and away.

Tense the muscles in your right foot again and hold the tension. Relax the foot, letting the tension run down, down and away.

Tense the muscles in your left foot, hold the tension for a few seconds before relaxing the foot and letting the tension run down through the sole of your foot into the ground and away.

Tense your left foot again. Hold the tension. Relax the foot, letting the tension run down, down and away.

Continue this exercise of tensing various muscle groups, holding the tension and then letting the tension run down through your body, your legs, your feet, into the ground and away. Repeat the exercise for each of the muscle groups below:

● right foot ● left foot ● right calf ● left calf ● right thigh ● left thigh ● bottom muscles ● stomach muscles ● chest muscles ● back muscles (relax each vertebra individually) ● right hand ● left hand ● right arm ● left arm ● right shoulder ● left shoulder ● neck muscles ● face muscles ● muscles on the back of your hand.

Once you have relaxed your whole body, focus your awareness on your breath coming in and going out at its own pace.

An extension to this exercise and one which can deepen your contact with ESSENTIAL YOU follows.

Focusing on past experiences

Walk back in your imagination to a time and place when you were in touch with ESSENTIAL YOU, a time when you felt at peace, whole and at one with the world around you. Ask yourself the following questions.

> Where were you?
> Who were you with?
> What were you doing?
> What were the colours around you?
> What were the sounds around you?
> What could you taste?
> What were the smells around you?
> What tactile sensations did you have?
> What were you feeling in your body?

Allow yourself two minutes to fully savour how it was for ESSENTIAL YOU then move on in time to another occasion when you felt essentially yourself and alive. Again, ask yourself

> Where were you?
> Who were you with?
> What were you doing?
> What were the colours around you?
> What were the sounds around you?
> What were the tastes around you?
> What were the smells around you?

What were the tactile sensations that you had?
What were you feeling in your body?

Allow yourself a further 2 minutes to experience ESSENTIAL YOU on this occasion.

Repeat the exercise a third time, exactly as above, then spend a minute or two focusing on your breath coming in and going out before opening your eyes. If you are working with a partner, relate to them what it is you have just experienced. If you are working alone, write down your experience. Pay particular attention to how you felt in your body at these times.

Most people feel more at peace with their body than usual. They notice they were more present, more aware of themselves, their feelings and their surroundings. For many it is as if the world has been washed clean and seen afresh for the first time. How was it for you?

There is no reason why you can't experience the energy, clarity, peace, joy and love of ESSENTIAL YOU all the time. I'm not promising that the path of change is easy or quick, but it is definitely possible. The place of ESSENTIAL YOU is a place of great strength, wisdom, insight, creativity and effortless energy. It is a place from which relating is easy, fruitful and alive. It's worth the effort of change.

Coming to terms with pain

In contacting ESSENTIAL YOU, we often inadvertently also contact WOUNDED YOU which can be painful. It's important therefore that we learn to come to terms with pain so that we can manage it. Pain can either be experienced physically or emotionally. The following exercises help us deal with both.

Most of us invest a great deal of time trying to avoid pain.

We like to believe that if we don't feel the pain it will go away. In fact it just goes underground where it causes stress, illness or depression. The Leboyer method of childbirth taught to expectant parents is a good example of how pain can be managed by simply breathing into it. This method encourages women in labour to breathe into their pain, thus alleviating the need for potentially dangerous pain–killing drugs.

These exercises are based on a similar philosophy, that pain is most easily handled by accepting and breathing into it.

1   Physical pain

If at any time you feel a pain in your body, a headache for instance or sore muscles, here are two constructive ways of dealing with the problem.

    a)   Visualise the pain in your mind.
How big is the pain?
How many centimetres long?
How many centimetres high?
What colour is the pain?
What shape is the pain?
Is it rough or smooth?
Is it hard or soft?
On a scale of 1 to 10,
    where 1 is the least painful,
    how bad is the pain?

Now repeat the exercise.

How big is the pain?
How many centimetres long?

How many centimetres high?
And so on.

Run through this exercise for as long as it takes for the pain to disappear.   This rarely takes more than two or three repetitions. People notice that on each repetition the pain reduces in intensity.

> b)   This time when you notice a pain, simply stop, sit as for the relaxation exercise and focus on your breath coming in and going out at its own pace.   Now notice where the pain is in your body.   Place your awareness on the pain and simply breathe into the pain.   You may notice that each time you do this the pain diminishes in intensity.

Pain is fuelled by denial, avoidance and fear.   It is released by acceptance and breath.

2   Emotional pain

Sit as for the relaxation exercise, concentrating on your normal flow of breath.
Now let a painful memory or emotion rise into your consciousness.   Let your attention move to your body.   Notice where the painful emotion rests in your body.   How big is it?   What flavour does it have?   Just let your awareness settle on the painful emotion and feel it fully.
Now ask your body to remember the earliest time you can remember experiencing this feeling.   Where were you?   Who were you with?   What were you doing?   What triggered your pain?   Feel how it was to be you at that time, experiencing this pain.   Notice what, if any, decision you made at this time about how you would

relate to life. Experience how you felt whilst making this decision.

Breathe into the pain in your imagination and ask it if it has anything it would like to tell you.

Then concentrate on your breath coming in and going out before slowly opening your eyes.

When doing this exercise many people find that once they develop a body awareness of something they thought was painful they realise that it wasn't as painful as they had at first thought. In fact they sometimes begin to wonder why I keep calling it pain when in fact now that they are experiencing it, it doesn't feel painful at all. Moreover, people are often amazed to find that if they repeat the exercise often they begin to notice patterns in their decision–making. There is a link between their early childhood decisions and their current behaviour and problems.

I have found that some leaders find these exercises more immediately useful than do others. For some it takes time and practice for them to be able to locate their emotions or to experience them. Practice does make it easier and it is worth the effort. Along with the painful emotions come the love, joy, peace and happiness that many of us have forgotten.

Chapter 3

Awareness And Acceptance—The Keys To Peaceful Chaos

Peter is one of the most remarkable leaders I have ever met. He is huge in stature, in vision and in heart. He has created around him an organisation that is a worldwide leader in its chosen area of manufacturing, its environmental policy and its social attitudes. His company has attracted international awards and recognition in these areas and has become a showpiece for its multinational parent.

Peter's company operates on the principle that the individual and their growth are the most important element to business success. If people keep growing and learning, Peter believes, the company can only continue to grow and learn along with them. Peter's company invests heavily in personal development for its staff, their families and the local community. The company has a crèche, a gym and supports the local community through its schools, hospital and welfare systems.

I started to work with Peter and his management team when they decided that their relationships had reached such a poor level that they were intolerable. Peter particularly was seen as the company's 'biggest asset and greatest problem'.

Peter's success belied his background. He had lost his father as an infant and had been fostered out to a number of families, but he returned to his mother when she remarried. His stepfather, however, didn't want to be reminded of Peter's father and so Peter was sent to a boarding school at the age of five.The boarding school was something worthy of a Dickens novel, complete with beatings, insufficient food and no affection.

This remarkable man made his way through school, university and the ranks of a large multinational. He gave all his immense energy and intelligence to his work at the cost of his marriage and many personal friendships. His satisfaction came from achieving results and improving the social conditions of those who depended on him. He personally championed personal development and music education in the local schools, a life–skills program for homeless youth and improved management of the local hospital.

All of the people reporting directly to Peter were married with families, and complained that keeping up with their boss precluded their having any personal life at all. When I first met them, many of Peter's managers were disgruntled and on the point of leaving despite their commitment to Peter's philosophy and achievements. Peter himself felt lonely, overburdened and resentful that everything seemed to emanate from and depend on him.

The unhappiness of the managers was aggravated by Peter's ferocious temper which flared up without warning. Peter later laughed that moving towards Peaceful Chaos had allowed his finger to grow back to its normal size after having been shortened by several centimetres from years of being stamped into tables.

Overwork and neglect were taking their toll on Peter's body. He had developed a serious illness that worried Peter only inasmuch as he feared it might slow him down in achieving his visions and spreading his ideas and successes to other organisations around the world.

When he first met me Peter was suspicious. What could I offer him when he was already so successful, and what did consultants know anyway? It was his managers who had called me in—he didn't see any big problems, and if only everyone would work a little harder and take a bit more responsibility everything would be fine.

What I was able to offer Peter was an opportunity to grow, move and heal; an opportunity to step back and allow himself to live. This process also created opportunities for those around Peter to grow into the space that he had vacated, thus allowing Peter to improve his relationships, enhance his peace of mind and increase the effectiveness of his company.

His managers reported that Peter became more human, more available and more real. Peter's temper abated, he was more approachable and his team gained confidence in his ability to support their decisions and actions. They were increasingly willing to assume responsibilities that Peter had previously kept for himself and to delegate to those below them. Peter thus provided a role model of change at the same time as creating opportunities, incentive and support for others to grow. Peter's health didn't significantly improve but his quality of life certainly did. He was able to devolve the day–to–day running of his operations to his managers and concentrate on his preferred areas of strategic development, leadership and public relations. He also had more time for his own development, relationship building, healing and enjoyment. For the first time in years Peter felt free to take an extended vacation, thus using some of the vast quantity of leave he had accumulated. The relationships in Peter's team were the most productive I have seen in a business setting. Not only was there next to no politicking, but managers actively relied on each other for practical and emotional support. The group became a multiskilled, strategic think tank and referred to themselves as a 'leadership support group'. Their international success continued to rise.

Addressing the real problems

Normally when people approach me to work with them in the area of change, what they are really asking me to do is help them find strategies, skills and understandings that will allow them to learn new and better ways of defending themselves against a changing environment.   My dilemma is that if I help people adapt their DEFENDED YOU, I am reinforcing their own unconscious patterns of fighting against reality.   I know that effective change happens when we open to reality, learn from and flow with it.   When we come from a position of defence our DEFENDED YOU becomes our driving force.   We operate out of our unconscious weakness rather than our conscious strength, unaware of what we are doing and why we are doing it.   We are blinded to the effects of our own actions, thoughts and emotions at the very time when perception and clear thinking are our strongest allies.

Most people when they envisage work–based change really have in mind some cosmetic surgery on their DEFENDED YOU. Their yearning is for the peace which they believe will come when the problems are fixed and go away.   Their inherent belief is that their lack of peace and discomfort is externally imposed, and if the external stimulus were to disappear so would the discomfort and unease. In other words, 'everything would be all right if only the world were different'.   The implication is that if you can change the world, and everybody in it, then you will feel better.

So DEFENDED YOU shifts its lines of defence and fortifies itself to change the environment, thus ignoring the fact that our discomfort and lack of peace comes from our own hot buttons, soft spots and unconscious wounds, not some present–moment external situation.   By strengthening DEFENDED YOU, we actually exacerbate our problems through distancing ourselves from the inner strengths and resources that lie in our ESSENTIAL YOU.

We thus stay within the limits of DEFENDED YOU and continually work from a reactive stance, wherein our potential and growth are restricted to learned, mostly unconscious defences.

Always defending from the rear, we fail to take the lead. While defending may provide short term success, it does so at the expense of our personal well-being, our ongoing relationships and our own growth.

The path to Peaceful Chaos lies through accessing and working with all the parts of ourselves. This means doing exactly the opposite to our habitual response. Like leaning down the mountain when skiing, doing our inner work feels unnatural and risky. We believe we don't have time and that the problems are outside us. We want to put our energies into changing others and the world, not looking at ourselves.

However, by coming to terms with what drives us, facing our inner fears and dealing with our own wounds, we are able to unleash our innate potential, thus ensuring that we find far better solutions to presenting problems. We thus grow through the experience and emerge richer, stronger and more successful as a result.

All we need is the awareness, courage and commitment to start and stay with the process, even when the going gets tough.

As you can imagine, offering people a change process that is exactly the opposite to what they believe is 'normal' is rarely an easy task. When most people face change they want less stress, less pain and quick answers. When the path offered is the antithesis of their habitual pattern and involves the discomfort of confronting repressed hurts, the resistance can be high. Moreover, as raising awareness is guaranteed to lead to an immediate increase in emotional discomfort, the characteristic response to real change is an immediate fortification of DEFENDED YOU, ensuring that we cut off access to our inner-strengths and knowing.

Following this pattern means we move from crisis to crisis, from patch-up change operation to patch-up change operation, convincing ourselves that the problem is the environment, other people and the rate of change. It's hard to admit that by concentrating on building up more and better defences we are working on the wrong problem. Through a mixture of ignorance and fear we sell ourselves short. We draw water from a rapidly draining well of DEFENDED YOU, completely missing the natural course, that is, ESSENTIAL YOU, that gushes some distance below our area of focus. We send out search parties, ration supplies and fight for what is left when all we have to do is go a little deeper to drink our fill.

Getting started

It is only in taking the time out to write this book that I was able to produce the model of DEFENDED YOU, WOUNDED YOU and ESSENTIAL YOU.   I have been using the components, insights, understandings and practical implications of the model for years but I had no model to explain myself to others. I simply knew in my heart that peace and success in times of rapid change lay in our essence, not in the tight, defended face we showed to the world. I also knew that to reach our essence we had to deal with the unhealed childhood hurts that lay in our unconscious. My problem was convincing other people who hadn't had my experience that the answer to their problems lay within them, as did the blocks to retrieving these answers.

Telling people who are almost totally focused on the external world that the work to be done lies in their emotions and unconscious minds is not easy. In many cases I haven't even tried. I simply helped people deal with their problems in a way that uncovered the DEFENDED YOU, supported them through the pain of WOUNDED YOU and strengthened their ESSENTIAL YOU.

The result of this was that my clients didn't understand why they simultaneously felt so terrible (WOUNDED YOU) and so wonderful (ESSENTIAL YOU), or why they were able to achieve results when working with me that they hadn't previously been able to achieve. They were also perplexed as to how they achieved these results when we seemed to be focusing on 'irrelevant issues' such as their feelings, their relationships, symbols, visualisations and 'the process'. I can't tell you how many times managers have demanded that we 'get on with it' ('it' being a presenting problem or task) and then been amazed that almost without reference to 'it' they had achieved more than they believed possible.

Back to Peter

Convincing Peter and his managers to try a new way of operating was not difficult. They were already leading–edge performers, they had already scoured the world for optimal solutions and they were convinced that if there were a known way to improve their situation they would already have found it. That I was offering them a journey into unknown territory presented them with a challenge. It also provided them with an opportunity to lead by exploring their own growth, and to provide a role model for a new way to lead.

Peter and his managers had already done a lot of personal development work and were open to the possibility they might be accomplices in their own difficulties. Moreover, they were ready to face and accept responsibility for any problems they encountered.

Working with such a team was a luxury. So many of us deny that we have any problems, discomforts or areas for improvement. By pretending everything is perfect or that problems have nothing to do with us, we avoid the necessity of investing time and energy in honestly facing the reality of our own attitudes, emotions and actions, and are provided with scapegoats for any problems or discomforts in our lives. These scapegoats become a perfect excuse to neglect our own growth and learning. Of course, this is all the unconscious work of DEFENDED YOU. While ever we can deny, avoid or project problems, we can stay blind to our own foibles, pains, misunderstandings and truths.

The strength of this defence is surprising. Time and again I have seen clients angrily deny pieces of information with which they had supplied me—even in writing—some minutes before.   I remember once working with the management team of a company in the throes of being bought out.   I was working with the top ten managers and divided them into two groups to look at the major problems facing them during the turbulent times at hand.   The group that didn't include the managing director reported back first with a list of 10 key problems.   On hearing this list the managing director rose to his feet and insisted that the group was making things up. 'We don't have those problems,' he insisted.   Nonplussed, the executives responded that they believed the problems were real and were similar to problems listed in two recent major consulting reports on the company.   'We do not have those problems,' repeated the managing director as he stormed out of the room, leaving us all stunned.

Time and again highly intelligent and successful leaders have told me they have no problems.   They have also told me there is no change.   I remember once being told by the head of a large and influential government department which had recently been halved that 'there was and never would be any change' in his department.

That Peter and his managers were prepared to admit that there was something to look at, that problems, change and improvement were possible, was rare.   That they were prepared to look at themselves as key players in the shaping of their own destiny was even rarer, particularly as they had decided to undertake the process as a team in a business setting. They had less difficulty than others in convincing themselves that they and their vision were worth the effort and discomfort of self–knowledge and growth.

The process

At this point it is important for you to know that what helped Peter and his team in their work with me was little affected by what we actually did. What worked and made the difference was not specific inputs of information, skills building or exercises. What mattered was the dynamics of the relationships, the personal shifts, emotions and insights, all of which rests firmly and privately in each individual's personal experience.   Change comes through each individual feeling, processing and opening to their experience.

In public life we place so much importance on what can be seen and measured that we usually miss the process. Yet in the process is the unfolding of life, change and learning. Process is the journey. We more often concentrate on the destination, the number of seats in the carriage and the cost of the fare rather than on the experience of travelling. So many of us see travel as a necessity to get from place to place rather than an opportunity to learn, appreciate new cultures, experiences and people.

Peaceful Chaos comes when we realise that life is a journey. Travelling is a personal experience. Your quality of work and private life depend on your ability to soak in and fully experience the journey.

Our journey

The journey that I took with Peter and his team was on many levels. Firstly, there was a physical journey. Together we set out to travel a long distance, in small boats, down a remote and intractable river. Secondly, there was a relationship journey. We navigated twists and turns in relationships, current and past, as we grew more real with each other and came closer together.   Thirdly, there were our personal internal journeys.   Each of us explored our inner strengths and weaknesses and discovered parts of ourselves we had long forgotten and denied. One manager wrote of the experience:

> I have learnt the value and necessity of 'reflective time' which allows me to keep pace with myself and my surroundings. I have learnt to look inside myself and to accept responsibility for me! I have learnt to concentrate on controlling those matters and things which are my responsibility. I have learnt the value of listening properly. I have learnt to respect the feelings of others. I have learnt the need to give timely and concise feedback. I have learnt the need, and how, to tell others exactly what I want and how I feel. I have learnt how to interact effectively with my team–mates and others.   I have learnt a lot about myself and my relationships with my team–mates. I have learnt how to deal with conflict. I have learnt to deal with my emotions. I now have a peace of mind which I enjoy and will work to keep that way.

I would like to tell you that I produced these outcomes by a carefully planned program of personal and interpersonal development. To do so would be lying.

When I was asked by Peter and his team to join them on their journey, I had no idea what to expect. I like being in nature but am not an outdoors expert. I had never taken a team on a team building expedition before and knew that to do so would take me right out of my territory. I was used to working in beautifully furnished conference rooms, complete with the latest electronic equipment. In this environment I was experienced, knew what to expect and was in control. Out in the bush I was a novice.

Unperturbed, I worked closely with Peter and his team

constantly clarifying what it was they wanted to achieve and how they would feel most comfortable achieving it. They employed an outdoors expert to organise and run the physical dynamics of the journey but the learning program rested with me.

I found that the team wanted to improve their strengths in a variety of areas which they were able to clearly articulate. Based on their input, I compiled a list of questions (see feedback questionnaire page 95 in this chapter) which we put to a number of their staff, colleagues and, in some cases, families to gauge how well the managers were doing on the areas they thought important. This information was fed back to the managers individually. For some there were unpleasant surprises, for others affirmation of a job well done. Either way, everybody learnt and benefited from the exercise.

I have found that, since most of us are heavily externally focused, a good place to start gaining information about ourselves is from external sources. In the beginning external feedback is a good source of information and impetus for change. As we develop our self–awareness, it becomes less important.

Another source of external information on which we drew was a commercial leadership preference indicator which helped the managers to see how their preferred work styles compared. From this, the managers saw that as a group they were open to exploration and change and preferred to work with concepts and projects rather than pay detailed attention to tasks. They realised that to complement the team they needed to put around them people who could help them follow through and implement their ideas.

Before beginning our physical journey, the managers, their partners and I also spent a day together learning some new skills in communication. We particularly concentrated on the use of 'I' statements (see page 88) and listening (see page 178, chapter 6). By the time we headed for the bush our personal and interpersonal journeys were well underway.

The starting point of our physical journey was a small town, home to a population that seemed to be able to be accounted for on one hand. The arrival of our party of 17 men and me changed the town's demography considerably.

Before leaving home the managers had decided that the trip would be 'dry'. We were probably one of the first 'teetotal' parties to visit the local pub.

On the nearby river we learnt to navigate and use the aluminium boats that awaited us there. We also learnt to erect our two-man tents and revived our bush-cooking skills. We were well prepared for the journey ahead.

We stayed one night in town and then, farewelled by the whole township (including two dogs to build up the numbers), we started our journey. The challenge in the physical expedition lay in in the difficulty of navigating in uncharted and highly changeable waters. No one had ever made the journey before.   The challenge of our interpersonal journey was to weld together a group of highly defended successful executives in a way that contributed to their personal growth and well-being and resulted in improved teamwork and company success.

Every day took on a familiar rhythm. We rose, built the fire, breakfasted, packed up camp and then met as a group to meditate. Initially, this practice met with some scepticism, but as time went on the managers began to feel and enjoy the benefits of 'slowing down long enough to catch up with themselves'. After our meditation we discussed both the physical and developmental aspects of the day ahead. We reviewed where we were going, how far we might travel and the location of the next fuel dump, along with our personal thoughts, feelings and plans.

Before the expedition I had envisaged that there would be large periods of time to work with the group as a whole and with individuals in depth. Within a few days of setting out, however, it became apparent that the distance we had set ourselves to travel and the time constraints many of us brought with us meant that time was scarce. I thus revised my expectations and asked each manager to work with his peers in boats as they travelled. Each manager was to give feedback to each of his peers and boss, based on the questionnaire devised for their staff. Moreover, this feedback was to be given using 'I' statements and the skills of listening they had learnt. On all occasions another manager or I was at hand to provide support, mediation and input where it was required. As there were four people to a boat, that meant at any one time in each vessel there was one manager giving feedback, one manager receiving it, one steering and navigating and one serving as a support person where needed.

The emphasis of people's attention differed according to the conditions at the time. When we were dodging trees, leading our boats through mud and tackling areas that were difficult to navigate, we let our feedback exercises go. When the course was clear and the conditions fine, we moved quickly through the feedback sessions.

The objectives of the expedition were clear. We were there to achieve the physical goal of being the first expedition to navigate this part of the river. We were also there to grow and learn as people, and to build the team. As such we shared the physical tasks and undertook to become safe people for each other to have around. My objective was to see each manager take responsibility for his own physical and emotional well–being and contribution to the team while simultaneously raising his personal awareness. We all learnt early on that being real was more important than anything.

After a day on the boats we pulled in to our camp, 3 hours before sunset. This allowed us to set up our camp site and tend our equipment in the light. We generally ate by the light of the campfire and then had an extended group session before bed.

The first night out, the only camp site we could find was

mud flats. It was impossible to erect our tents and we all stood ankle deep in mud. We very quickly found out who snored and who didn't. The ice broke early.

When the expedition began it was very important to the managers that we covered the full distance. As time passed and we began to experience the benefits of life in the wilderness and of growing interpersonal intimacy, where we were going became of less and less importance. This was lucky because we began to see that although we had allocated 10 days for the journey it's successful completion was more likely to take us 2 weeks, time that many of us just didn't have.

Building ESSENTIAL YOU

I have found that it is impossible to be in a beautiful or imposing natural setting without being touched by the awe of nature. For each person this is experienced in a different way, but nobody is left unmoved. The longer that we stayed in the wilderness, the harder it was for any of us to keep up our defences and the easier it was for each one to contact our ESSENTIAL YOU. We each let in the magnificence of the natural world around us. We all marvelled at the pelicans and other water birds that proliferated along the river banks. We noticed the miles and miles of open country, stretching beyond our gaze. We saw paw prints at our feet when we woke and watched dingoes swimming near out boats. We drank in the magnificent colours of the sun rising and setting against the grandeur of a near–desert landscape.

It was impossible for any of us to stay stuck in our DEFENDED YOU. How could any of us not notice that we were more than a set of learned defences? We all basked in the wonder of nature and began to contact our inner strength as part of the bigger scheme of things.

Our daily meditations enhanced this process and we started to move some of the unconscious blocks and contact the depth of well–being, openness, relationship, clarity and peace that lay beneath them. In the evenings we used our group sessions as an opportunity to gain insights into specific issues and problems that had faced us during the day. Together we created an environment in which it was safe for us to let down our barriers and talk from our heart and soul. We began to see each other as real people with emotions, defences, wounds and inner treasures that had previously been hidden or we had failed to notice.

Emotional safety

The effect of the wilderness, the meditations, the growing intimacy and accumulating feedback was that our DEFENDED YOU began to give way to a depth of feeling that many were surprised to find underneath. Peter and his team began to experience the pain of WOUNDED YOU. The strengthening of our ESSENTIAL YOU provided each of us with renewed inner strength but we still had a lot of pain and discomfort with which to deal.

We did this by creating a safe environment, an environment in which each individual was encouraged, supported and validated for being real. Real people have emotions. They laugh, cry, feel sad, happy, confused, in awe and despairing. They have doubts, joys, fears and triumphs. Real people are emotionally healthy and have sufficient confidence in themselves and others to let others see who they are.

Creating a safe environment has very little to do with anything that we did. Safety comes from being around safe people.

Safe people are those who are themselves real, who are emotionally comfortable with themselves, warts and all.   Safe people listen, really listen.   They validate you and your emotions, they set their limits and encourage you to set yours.   Safe people don't try to fix you up, advise you, counsel, heal or teach you.   They know you are capable of doing all that for yourself.   Safe people stay open and available around you while you explore your own issues, your own questions and your own answers.   Safe people are nutritious people—their face lights up when you enter the room and they have no plans for your improvement.

I have spent the last 10 years developing the ability to be a safe person.   I can only say that it is the most difficult thing I have ever undertaken.   It has made all my previous studies appear simple and somewhat irrelevant by comparison.   The journey I have been through is long and varied, but a key element of it was a decision that I couldn't help anyone else until I had my own act in order.   Moreover, the best way I could help another person was to be real, human, open and available.   It was up to others what use they made of my humanity.   In other words, I accepted my own dictum that you cannot change another person. You can provide a role model, support, encouragement and shared experience: it is up to others what they do with that.   If and how they change is their responsibility.

From this stance it is hard for me to tell you exactly how we created the safety for people to deal with their WOUNDED YOU. My experience of it was that I listened and encouraged others to do the same.   I never tried to teach, fix up, advise or heal anyone, I simply shared my humanity and encouraged others to follow my lead.   I congratulated people on being real while supporting any decisions to withhold the expression of emotions or thoughts when an individual felt to reveal them would be too exposing or risky.   I noticed that the managers soon offered each other the same level of support and safety.

Nobody was forced to do anything or follow any group norms. Everybody was encouraged to be true to themselves and their own judgements, and everybody was congratulated when that judgement lead to them sharing a little more of themselves with the group.

For me it was like watching flowers open in spring. I saw the crusty walls of years of political infighting fall away and be replaced with a level of friendship and intimacy that I'm sure will last a lifetime.

One of my most vivid memories relates to my own learning in the area of emotional safety. Repeatedly during the trip I suggested to the managers that the way to raise their awareness and heal their wounded child selves was to feel their emotions and express them to safe people. I insisted that the aim of this exercise wasn't to get the other person to change but to strengthen their own resources and grow in a way that would lead to closer, more nourishing relationships. I also stressed that listening is just that. It is the skill of hearing how it was for another without feeling you have to do something about it.

Often during the day we would need to take our bearings and would group all the boats together while we compared map readings and discussed navigational details. On one occasion Peter wanted us to know that he thought we were travelling too fast. Earlier we had made a group decision that any changes in navigation would be discussed by the whole group. This day several major decisions had been made by those in the leading boats without reference to the others. Peter, not being in one of the faster boats, had not been party to these decisions. He wanted us all to know that he felt disappointed that we hadn't kept to our agreements.

Failing to take notice of any of my own counsel I started to propose a whole range of suggestions to help Peter feel more in control. Did he want to move to a faster boat? Did he want us to change our policy? Did he want us to review our decisions? In spite of all my efforts at appeasing Peter's disappointment he grew angrier and angrier. The angrier he got, the more suggestions I threw up to help him to feel better.

Eventually in desperation Peter looked at me and said, 'You told us to express how we felt. That is what I am doing. I don't want anything to be different, I just wanted you to hear my feelings.' There, in front of everyone, I was shown that no matter how far down this road we travel, we always have further to go. Peter had spent some time prior to this session with his team-mates practising expressing how he felt. They had supported him to take the risk of letting us know how it was for him. I had failed to listen. Luckily I, like everybody else, am able to learn from my mistakes.

Completing the journey

Learn we all did; from our mistakes, from our growing awareness, from our increased connection with our inner essence and from each other. One of our major discoveries was that people and things change.

When we realised that it was going to take more than 10 days to reach our destination, many of the group were disappointed. To some, the physical completion of the trip mattered dearly, their hearts were set on the expedition's achievement. Others realised that they had received so much from the team building and personal development side of the trip they actually no longer cared about reaching the end point. They decided they had already received more than they thought possible. Covering the distance was the icing on the cake, nice but not necessary. At this stage someone suggested that for an expedition to be successful only some members need to reach the goal. As those members of the party who were keenest to keep going also happened to be those with less restricted time limits, we decided to delegate the expedition's success.

This simple decision was a landmark for the team. It was an early expression of trust and creative thinking that was to characterise the team from then on. It was a recognition that everybody can win by supporting people to make their own decisions and follow their own best course. Trust, teamwork, communication and strategic thinking can ensure that the impossible can be achieved without any losers.

Those of us who chose to return home on schedule were driven out from our camp site by a local landholder. It took several hours driving to get us from the river back to 'civilisation', a small station house on a dusty highway. The landowner was curious as to what we had been doing so far from home. I told him of our journey and its objectives. 'Oh, I understand,' he commented. 'It's like my oxen. If I hook 'em up in the same direction they can move mountains. But hook 'em up in opposite directions and they get ya nowhere.'

The next journey

The depth of the experience we shared was beyond anything I have been able to convey on paper. However it was sufficiently meaningful to lead to real change for us all. One Manager wrote of the experience one year later:

> I have been involved in a process of transformation [which has] influenced the way I treat myself, respond/react to others

and [which has] helped to strip away the superficial behaviour and posturing which was prevalent within our team. Today I find I am more caring of myself and others. I am supporting and supported by others within my team. I have found enormous relief from not being burdened with superficial detail. This has given me enormous satisfaction and success in dealing with issues in a far great depth than previously.

Another concluded, 'The next trip has already begun.' That trip was taking all this learning back into the hurly–burly of the workplace and the busy everyday life of each manager.

A number of things supported this transition.

1   The managers had experienced on a deep level real, as against superficial, change. They were deeply committed to maintaining the development of their ESSENTIAL YOU, continuing to manage their DEFENDED YOU and working on healing their WOUNDED YOU.

2   They had ascertained for themselves that the success of their organisation, their teams and their own careers rested on their ability to be whole, fully functioning human beings.

3   They had found within themselves answers to many of their problems and had experienced that operating another way was well worth the effort.

4   They made a commitment to an ongoing program of personal growth and development, linked to the strategic needs of their company. They decided to lead by living the message, and

the message they wanted to live was one of development, growth and rapid change.

5   As part of this they decided to create around them a safe environment in which others could also grow and change. The managers realised that to do this they needed to move further down the path of creating themselves as safe people.

Despite my inability to clearly articulate what the next steps might be, the end of phase one resulted in a commitment by the managers to work with me two days a month for the following year. They didn't know what to expect from this commitment but they were prepared to trust their own judgement and feelings and take the risk. Seeing the results and the company's ongoing success, I can only assume that the risk paid off.

'I' statements

The following 'I' statements, feedback questionnaire and guided visualisation were integral in leading to a successful expedition. I include them here for your use.

'I' statements are a common element of any basic communication or negotiation course. They are used in parenting programs, relationship counselling, assertiveness training and basic supervision courses. They come in many forms. The form I use is excellent for helping to gain awareness of DEFENDED YOU and WOUNDED YOU.

Step 1 involves clearly and objectively describing an incident that actually happened. For example, '**When you told me at the meeting last Tuesday that you were disappointed that**

I hadn't finished the quality survey on time...'

Step 2 involves stating how you felt about the incident. For example, **'I felt confused.'**

Step 3 involves saying what you would like to do about the situation and/or your feelings. For example, **'And what I would like is that I learn to express my priorities to you in advance so that I can be more realistic in my commitments.'**

The important thing is that Step 1 is an objective description, Step 2 is a clear statement of your emotions offered without judgement or blame and that Step 3 is a statement of what you are going to do about the situation.

This apparently simple form of language has within it a huge amount of learning. 'I' statements properly used can increase our self-awareness, our quality of relationship, our organisational team work, our peace of mind and our strategic leadership. It sounds a lot I know but I swear it is true.

Let's look at some of the benefits that flow from using 'I' statements.

'I' statements assist people to focus on what actually happened, to focus on the reality rather than a half-baked illusion. Usually when we talk we are so vague that it is difficult to discover what has happened and the effect it has had. I have noticed that even highly trained leaders and professionals have great difficulty in stating honestly and openly what they witnessed or experienced. (The police often find this when attempting to gather evidence from eye-witnesses.)

When we start to focus on what is actually happening we begin to notice, to be present and to face reality head on. We are all so quick to judge others and their behaviour that we often distort the facts with our own opinions. So we say things like, 'When you lost your temper and dumped on me...' rather than, 'When you said you were disappointed...'. We know what he said because we heard him, but we don't know that he lost his temper or that he dumped on us, it is merely our opinion. By providing a clear description of what we believe happened, we give other people the chance to decide whether they agree with our version of the truth. By making that statement as objective as possible we avoid alienating our listener and encourage them to join us in an exploration of the situation under discussion. This helps both to solve any problems and to build the relationship.

Very often people present their opinions as facts. They say things like, 'The fact is...' or, 'The reality is...' and then present their opinion as if it were the only truth. Experts back their opinions up with a plethora of figures and other people's opinions just to prove they are right. We all use a range of defences to coerce and manipulate others into accepting and agreeing with our version of the truth. 'I' statements are a way of encouraging us not to do that. Moreover, by forcing us to report what did happen or is happening, they encourage us to notice the dynamics of life, relationship and action that is going on around us.

'I' statements stop people hiding behind their language. So often people talk in terms of 'we', 'you', 'the bank', 'the company', 'senior management', 'the government', 'the unions' or 'Everybody knows...' that it is hard to find out what the speaker actually feels and thinks. This, of course, allows the speaker to avoid any responsibility for their communication. If the problem lies with an outsider or group of outsiders, the speaker is powerless to do anything but comment, complain and give advice—none of which will help anyone in any way, improve the situation or lead to real change.

When people begin to talk in terms of 'I' they start to raise their awareness as to how they feel, what they think and what they would like to have happen.   It is only through awareness and responsibility that we will begin to enrich our lives, deal successfully with change and begin to reach our full potential individually and collectively.

'I' statements help us bring our emotions to our awareness.One of DEFENDED YOU's strongest ploys is to deaden our emotions and then convince us that emotions don't matter, are inappropriate or that they don't exist.   The use of 'I' statements' puts emotions on the table and lets us recognise them and deal with them. For many people this is a particularly threatening thing to do.   I have engaged in long battles with groups of executives, sometimes for hours, as to the value of dealing with emotion.

There is an interesting belief in our society that emotions are subjective, personal matters that have nothing to do with the world of work.   And yet from my experience they have everything to do with it.   Take a minute to think about the behaviour of the people with whom you have worked over the years.   How much of their behaviour would you say is entirely rational and how much of it is emotionally driven?   Think particularly of stressful situations and you will see behaviour that can hardly be called objective or rational.

Emotion in and of itself is what makes us human.   It is a source of great energy, learning and   strength.   What causes the problems is repressed emotion, denied emotion and hidden emotion. In other words the problem isn't the emotion but DEFENDED YOU which is doing its best to ensure that we don't experience, recognise and deal appropriately with our feelings.

It's by going against the dictates of DEFENDED YOU and acknowledging at least to ourselves how we feel that we begin to bring the hidden drivers of the 'old brain' into our conscious awareness and take more responsibility for and control over our lives. It is from this stance that problems get solved, relationships are built and lives work.

Peter and his managers were amazed to find as they became more conscious that acting out of their unconscious emotions they had actually created a large percentage of the problems they thought were external to them. 'In fact,' one manager wrote later, 'we were becoming flat, disinterested and fragmenting whenever the level of crises was significantly reduced and would [unconsciously] leave mundane tasks until they became crises.'

It is true that in some situations expressing how we feel is opening WOUNDED YOU to attack. These situations are fewer, however, than most of us think. A non–judgemental expression of our emotional reaction to a situation has a surprising ability to build bridges between people. It's almost as if we recognise each other's essence and open to the opportunity of real connection and relationship. There is, however, always a risk, and all risks require judgement based on a personal assessment of the situation and an ability to bear the consequences.

That we take this risk very rarely is always brought home to me when I notice the paucity of people's language when it comes to stating how they feel. On one occasion I banned the use of 'good', 'fine' and 'OK' because they were the only words people seemed to have to describe their emotions.   As humans we are capable of thousands of emotions. Below are listed just a few.

•	accepting	•	exhausted
•	aggressive	•	exuberant
•	anxious	•	frustrated
•	bored	•	frightened
•	cautious	•	grieving
•	cold	•	guilty

- curious
- delighted
- determined
- disappointed
- enraged
- envious
- lonely
- surprised

- happy
- hungover
- hurt
- inspired
- jealous
- relaxed
- suspicious
- withdrawn

So 'I' statements help us acknowledge to ourselves how we feel and then, based on our level of courage and assessment of appropriateness, allow us to build our relationships by expressing our feelings to others.

'I' statements help us work out what we want. If people have problems with noticing what is actually happening and how they feel about it, they have no less difficulty in working out what they want. Most of us are so used to shifting our responsibility and power outward that we have actually lost touch with our ability to decide what we want and what we are going to do about what we want. I was shocked when I first became aware of this tendency in myself. I remember thinking that my ability to be clear about my own needs, wants and desires was like an arm that had been in plaster and the muscles responsible for decision and action needed to be retaught how to operate.

I have seen so many leaders stumble when asked what they wanted to do about a situation about which they had strong feelings. Some people have trouble simply working out what they want, what solution they desire. Others have no difficulty deciding what they want, their problem is that what they want invariably involves other people/situations changing or being different. They always want the same thing—for reality to be other than the way it is.

'I' statements empower us to create ourselves as the solution.

'I' statements therefore present an opportunity for us to come to terms with the reality that the only person over whom we have any control is ourselves. We cannot force another person to think or feel or act any way but the way they choose to think, feel or act. We can apply pressure, we can manipulate, we can nag, bully and threaten, but the choice is always with the other person. Moreover, everything has a consequence and if we expend our efforts trying to force others to be the way we want them to be, not only are we unlikely to succeed but we have every chance of receiving a strong and unwanted backlash, usually made all the more awkward because it is covert, cumulative and unconscious.

'I' statements provide the perfect tool for us to rethink how we relate to others and to the world in general. They encourage us to take responsibility for our own feelings, thoughts and actions, thus freeing others to do the same. They allow us to put forward ourselves as the solution, thus providing others with a choice as to how they will react. When we create ourselves as a solution and therefore a role model, it is surprising how many people choose to follow our lead, saving us the huge amount of energy and stress that we usually invest in trying to force, coerce, manipulate and entice—often without even realising what we are doing.

'I' statements' as process not content

When looking back at my journey with Peter and his team it is hard to believe that a program based around one questionnaire and one language tool would keep high-powered, action-oriented managers interested for such a long period, and that such a small amount of 'content' would lead to so much benefit, but it did.

Through the process of using 'I' statements the managers became aware how often they failed to recognise or acknowledge their emotions, and began to realise the frequency with which they acted out of unconscious drives that were often counterproductive to the situation at hand, their relationships and themselves. They began to notice how much of their energy they put into trying to manipulate and control others instead of taking responsibility for their own well–being, interests and actions. They also took note of how successful they had been in hiding these things from themselves. They began to see how their language assisted them in remaining unconscious, and how their unconsciousness had helped them to stay defended, alienated and disempowered.

The strength of the emotions that were uncovered during this exercise was surprising as was the willingness of each person to express and share these emotions. As time passed and the defences fell away, people started to relate to each other in ways that they had never before experienced. Things that appeared to be problems in the past were no longer seen as problems, rifts in relationships began to mend and old wounds started to heal. We all came to the conclusion that what matters is not winning or being right but learning, growing, relating and being open to life. From this stance everything is easier, life is fuller, relationship possible and success deeper, richer and more clearly targeted.

Feedback questionnaire

Communication skills

Listening for meaning.
(Do you believe that the manager hears what you say?)

Establishing empathy.
(Do you feel he understands you and your needs?)

Resolving conflict.
(Do you feel he is confident and skilled in resolving conflict?)

Being appropriately assertive.
(Does he make his point clearly while respecting the perspective of others?)

Relationship skills

Establishing rapport.
(Do you feel at ease in his presence?)

Creating win–win outcomes
(Does he make everyone a winner?)

Building trust.
(Do you trust him?)

Managing emotions.
(Does he deal constructively with your feelings and with his own?)

Team–building skills

Recognising and building on strengths.
(Does he see and support your strengths?)

Understanding other's contribution.
(Does he understand and value your role in the team?)

Developing interdependence and team flexibility.
(Does he share information appropriately with you and support you to develop in your areas of responsibility?)

Consulting others and enlisting their cooperation.
(Does he seek your opinion and act on it?)

Strategic skills

Does he set clear objectives?

Does he let you know his objectives and how they affect you?

Does he prioritise objectives and tasks appropriately?

Does he communicate these priorities clearly to you?

Does he develop action plans to implement objectives?

Does he follow through decisions?

Does he learn from his mistakes?

Does he learn from his successes?

Are there any further comments you would like to make?

A guided visualisation

My experience is that for people to gain maximum benefit from a guided visualisation they need to relax first. You will therefore find the beginning of this exercise is the same as the relaxation exercise on page 62, chapter 2.

Step 1 Sit comfortably in a chair, ensuring that both feet are firmly on the ground. If you are wearing high heels take them off. Some people prefer to lie down, with their knees bent and their feet on the ground. The only problem with this is that it increases your chances of going to sleep. Nodding off can reduce the effectiveness of the meditation, and if you are working in a group and you snore it can be disruptive to others.

Step 2 Close your eyes and cup your hands in your lap.

Step 3 Tense the muscles in your right foot. Hold the tension for a few seconds and then relax, letting the tension run down through your foot into the ground and away.

Tense the muscles in your right foot again. Hold the tension. Relax the foot, letting the tension run down, down and away.

Tense the muscles in your left foot. Hold the tension for a few seconds then relax the foot, letting the tension run down through the foot into the ground and away.

Tense the left foot again. Hold the tension. Relax the foot, letting the tension run down through the foot into the ground and away.

Continue this exercise of tensing various muscles, holding the tension and then letting the tension run down through your body, your legs, your feet, into the ground and away. Repeat the exercise with each of the muscle groups below.

right foot
left foot
right calf
left calf
right thigh
left thigh
bottom muscles

stomach muscles
chest muscles
back muscles (relax vertebra by vertebra)
right hand
left hand
right arm
left arm
right shoulder
left shoulder
neck muscles
face muscles
the muscles on the back of your head

Step 4 Once you have relaxed the whole body, begin to concentrate on your breath coming in and going out at its own pace... in and out at its own pace. You can then meditate on your breath for as long as you feel comfortable.

Step 5 Shift your awareness from your breath to create a picture of yourself in your imagination, standing in a sunny meadow. Notice the flowers, trees and vegetation around you. Drink in the colours, the sounds, the sensations and the emotions of being in a sun–filled meadow. As you stand there a sunbeam begins to cover you, and you stand encased in its light, warmth and glow.

From this place of light and warmth see yourself move in your imagination to your 'place of peace'. This is your private place, a place where you feel at home, at one with yourself and your surroundings. For most people their peaceful place is somewhere in natural surroundings, on a mountain, by a lake or near the sea. For many they are places they have visited or composites of favourite holiday or recreation spots.

Look around your 'peaceful place', soak in the beauty, the

peace and the joy. Notice the colours, the sounds, the movements, the shapes, the sensations and the tastes. Really enjoy your place of peace.

Spend 5 to 10 minutes enjoying your 'place of peace' in your own way.

When you are ready to return to the present say goodbye to your 'peaceful place' and remember that it is your place in your imagination and that you can return there any time you want.

Step 6 See yourself move back to the meadow and into the beam of light. Feel its healing warmth and know that you can have that feeling of peace and wholeness whenever you chose.

Then return your concentration to your breath coming in and going out at its own pace. Gently, in your own time, open your eyes.

Having worked with many groups of executives as they use this meditation technique, I am always struck by the difference in people's energy when they return from their 'peaceful place'. A quiet calm pervades the room and people begin to think and relate differently.

I have found that by using meditation techniques, such as the one outlined, during business–planning and problem–solving sessions, that we are able to achieve far superior results in much less time than if we only concentrate on the business at hand. Once people become present with themselves and each other, and once they start to really think, problems seem to solve themselves remarkably quickly.

Many of my clients find that the above meditation works better in a group. They find that when they are alone they have trouble inducing the same level of peace and calm they experienced with the group. They find, however, that relaxation and meditation tapes can overcome some of these problems. They also find other methods of meditation that work for them.

One of my clients has a 'quiet corner' in his house. This 'quiet corner' has his comfortable chair positioned to look out the window. He finds sitting and looking, thinking or reading quietly has a meditative effect on him. Other clients like to go and sit on the beach, or in the bush, and just be. One fellow I met who had particular trouble sitting and meditating found his own novel solution. He used to run along the beach with his eyes closed, just within the water's edge so that he didn't lose his way or bump into anything.

There is no 'correct' way to meditate. It is purely a matter of finding the method that works for you. The aim is to clear your mind so that you can think, slow down and catch up with yourself, so that you can be present. A friend of mine was told by her brother, who was a farmer, that he didn't go in for all that meditation stuff. He was, however, rather partial to leaning on the fence looking at the cows.

It's all a matter of taste.

Chapter 4

Strategy In Motion

When I first met Ian he had recently been appointed to one of the most prestigious management positions in the country. He was in his early forties and had a brilliant track record in what was known to be a very cutthroat industry. He surprised me with his openness to learning, new ideas, people and change. I was so used to chief executives who on first meeting presented me with their hardened DEFENDED YOU, leaders who through years of playing politics had learned that the only safe way to approach any new person, particularly a consultant, was with caution and suspicion. I was expecting someone who denied that they had any problems, any vulnerability or any need to grow and learn. Ian took me aback.

He was relaxed, searching and available. He had a problem and he wanted help in solving it. As the new chief executive of Palmers, the country's leading company in a service-based industry, he had inherited not only a well-established and highly respected position but a company with a culture that was not greatly changed since its inception last century. His lieutenants and staff were highly technically trained, top quality people. The organisation had a well-defined market niche that had been supported by a virtual monopoly created by government regulation and the difficulty of competitors establishing credibility with Palmers' conservative customer base.

The people at Palmers worked hard, were very status conscious, highly task focused and not keen to change.

But there had been change. Competitors, supported by changes in federal legislation, were eating their way into the company's market, laying Palmers open to real competitive threat for the first time in their history. This had led to a major organisational restructure and the loss of about 20 per cent of jobs, mainly through voluntary redundancy. Moreover, it was becoming increasingly obvious that success for Palmers would be strongly linked to their ability to incorporate and innovate around leading–edge computing systems. Having come from a highly customer–oriented background, Ian was further aware that Palmers had to focus its culture more on the wants and needs of the customers and less on the technical expertise of the staff. He was also convinced that change had to be a way of life at Palmers, not just a series of one–off occurrences. Ian's experience and exposure to worldwide trends convinced him that change was the only thing of which he and his company could be absolutely sure in the coming decade.

Where Ian had problems was in having the people who worked for him share his understanding, his vision and embrace change.

Ian was one person, a new boy at that. He was greatly outnumbered by a management and workforce who had been playing a game by rules established last century, rules that had worked well and although beginning to show signs of strain still kept Palmers in an enviable position. Ian was fighting for future excellence while his people were still basking in yesterday's success.

The process we undertook together was what we called strategy. I make no claims that what we did was technically correct or textbook perfect. What we did was combine the need to scan and analyse the environment and make strong business decisions with the need to move a large and well–established organisation and all its people through many stages of development. This resulted in an organisation staffed by people who could continually scan, analyse and make decisions in a changing environment; people who had the personal, interpersonal and organisational skills necessary to adapt themselves to their changing environment whilst working with their environment so that it adapted to them. In other words, we combined what is normally called strategy formulation, with what is normally called strategy implementation, with what is normally called organisational change. We came up with an organisation run by people who understood that change is the only constant, that business success depends on accurate and current information, astute analysis, courageous decision–making and the human ability to grow and change as a way of life.

This is what I call **strategy in motion.**

Strategy as a way of being

Strategy is a way of being—not a piece of paper.

When I was at business school, like all budding managers we were taught to plan, organise, control and evaluate. We were instructed in the arts of scientific method, statistical analysis, forecasting and operations management. We learnt about industry analysis, strategic planning and behaviour modification.

Implicit in all this was the belief that we could predict the future from the past, rationally determine what was the most desirable course to take and then modify the behaviour of the people around us so that they would play the part we needed them to play to achieve our plan.

It all sounded so good in theory: it made us feel so powerful and in control. What a pity it doesn't work.

Reality, it seems, isn't as logical as business school theory.

Firstly, things change at such a rate that by the time you've analysed the environment, devised your strategies and put in place the structures and systems you need to implement your plan, the world has changed and you're out of date.

Secondly, people just don't fit into nice neat formulae, projections and action plans.

Change

We live in a highly complex system that is in a state of constant instability and chaos. Although basic truths rarely change, the reality of our day–to–day existence changes dramatically. Who would have predicted the fall of eastern Europe, the rise of the computer or the success of the Biro. My mother grew up with a drip safe to cool her food, a kerosene lamp to light her house and a horse and buggy to take her where she wanted to go. Today she drives an automatic car, uses a microwave oven and a CD player and receives computer–written letters and cheques.

Anyone who predicted the amount of change that has occurred this century would have been labelled a dreamer, their 'visions' would have been assigned to the world of science fiction, fantasy or soothsaying. I remember reading Peter Drucker on his early association with Tom Watson, the Founder of IBM. Drucker had difficulty getting his article on Watson published because the editor thought Watson to be a madman. Watson was talking about artificial intelligence long before anyone understood what it was.

As a society we have a bias in favour of what we know and a predilection to certainty. We want someone to tell us how it is going to be in the future but want their predictions to be based on things with which we are already comfortable. We don't want to have to make the adjustments that are necessitated by radical change. We so much want the security of knowing that we will latch on to and believe plans based on past certainties, while we fight hard to deny or even destroy emerging evidence and thought that leads us in entirely new directions.

Tolstoy wrote:

> I know that most men, including those at ease with problems of the greatest complexity, can seldom accept even the simplest and most obvious truth if it be such as would oblige them to admit the falsity of conclusions which they have delighted in explaining to colleagues, which they have proudly taught to others and which they have woven thread by thread into the fabric of their lives.

James Gleik, in recalling the history of the now well–accepted chaos theorists, wrote:

> Every scientist who turned to chaos theory early has a story to tell of discouragement or open hostility. Graduate students were warned that their careers could be jeopardised if they wrote theses in an untested discipline, in which their advisers had no expertise... To some the difficulty of communicating new ideas and the ferocious resistance from traditional quarters showed how revolutionary the new science was.

This resistance to new ideas and change poses leaders with two key problems. Firstly, it blinds strategists not only to radical and emerging change but to the possibility of unforeseen change, and, secondly, it makes change difficult to implement within organisational ranks.

People will be people

Unlike the 'rational man' that my professors told me populated organisations, I found that real people lie, cheat, hide information, play politics, withhold their effort, steal the company silver, glue the boss's ruler to the desk and phone his wife to let her know that he is having an affair and he is doing it now—name, address and telephone number supplied. When people are frightened, alienated or feeling manipulated they steal the stationery, leak information to the press and get sick. They daydream, spread rumours and make mistakes. They do just about everything but what you have planned for them to do.

All these human idiosyncrasies are the result of people operating unconsciously out of DEFENDED YOU. They are more likely to do that when they feel frightened. Fear is a normal response to change but many managers use fear as the basis of their management style. They use their power over rewards and punishments as a way of coercing people to comply with their wishes. While this appears to work in the short–term in the longer term it results in the kind of crazy behaviour I have outlined above.

Of course, when people *do* behave as frightened people will, their defensive behaviour triggers the DEFENDED YOU of their boss who intensifies his or her defensiveness, thus ensuring an ongoing, lose–lose, downward–spiralling power struggle. Both sides believe that they can't change their own behaviour because of the defensiveness of the other. In other words, everybody abdicates responsibility for the defensive behaviour of the other while at the same time claiming that they themselves must defend to protect themselves. Each sees themselves as a victim of the bad behaviour of the other, fortifies their DEFENDED YOU and fights to survive. This is a perfect way to ensure that nothing and nobody changes.

The boss waits for the staff to be more 'cooperative' and the staff wait for the boss to be more 'reasonable'—a stalemate is reached and becomes 'the way we do things around here'.

A technique I often use when working with executives who complain that their staff won't change according to plan is to ask the executives how they feel when someone tries to get them to change, to behave in a way determined by the other. The responses include get angry, resist, argue, walk out, get even, go quiet, do nothing, and undermine the other's position. Nobody, it seems, likes to have others determining how they should act, think or be. Very few people like change, even fewer people like change when they feel it is the result of manipulation by another rather than as a natural consequence of the environment in which they live. In other words, people dislike change. They hate being controlled.

Strategy versus planning

Gerry Johnson, in his study of the development of strategy in three firms over a period of 12 months, concluded that strategy formulation (planning) is usually 'incremental and adaptive' and, as such, 'limited in the extent to which [it is] able to assist in the process of managing'. He went on to say, 'it has become clear that we need to place strategic decision–making in a political context'.

Michael Porter, the author of *Competitive Strategy,* later wrote: 'Strategic planning has fallen out of fashion. In most companies it has not contributed to strategic thinking.'

What both these authors are alluding to is the failure of traditional planning to keep pace with the reality of rapid change or to take into account the dynamics of human interaction or personality.

Highly rational, content–centred planning that results in a

static, detailed plan simply doesn't work. Strategy is a way of being, a way of thinking and a way of relating. In short, strategy is a process of learning, acting, deciding and communicating. It is iterative, human, continuous, messy, chaotic and holds huge, rarely tapped potential.

Strategy in motion is the art of having the people who make up an organisation working towards their joint success through staying open to and capitalising on change as it happens. This is a very human process. What matters is not that you get the perfect answer, the ideal plan or the best−reasoned analysis but that you are tuned in to the process of business, relationship and life that is going on around you, that you are conscious of your own part in that process and that you learn from everything that happens. I have a practice of congratulating my clients on their failures. Not because I particularly admire calamity but because it is in noticing what works and what doesn't work that we learn.

In times of rapid change, what matters is not getting things right but staying open to, noticing and learning from everything that happens, and more particularly to grow as human beings from our experience of life.

Most planning is done as a rational exercise by people operating out of their DEFENDED YOU. It takes no account of the fact that to have the strategy implemented, and therefore work, you have to gain the cooperation and support of many people. Most plans are in fact written as a defence against change and against relationship. They are written in isolation from the people who will have to make them work. Moreover, they are written on yesterday's data without a full embracing of today's realities, relationships and dreams. They are a means of control, not a means to success.

Unfortunately, plans often become a prescription for an organisation's operations. Fearing that their success will be judged against their ability to keep on plan, on budget and on time, people limit their success to what was thought rational by the planner at the time the plan was written. When the goal becomes keeping to the plan, unforeseen opportunities become unwise diversions; new events are often seen as problems, nuisances or 'contingencies' because they are different from what was expected. Conflicts of interests and differing perspective are seen as blocks to achieving the target, that is, the plan. From this stance a large part of what happens is seen as inconvenient because it doesn't comply with how someone thought the future should be. Despite the fact that things change and the future is unseeable, people in organisations that are plan driven spend all their time trying to force reality to fit the plan, thus wasting a huge amount of time and energy. When people are the centre of our efforts, in forcing reality to be 'as planned' we also run the risk of triggering their defences and undermining, even endangering, our relationships.

When reality refuses to fit the plan, people in 'plan driven' organisations go looking for a scapegoat, someone or something to blame for things not turning out 'as they should'. What they completely overlook is that reality will go on being the way it is and people will be themselves ad infinitum. The trick isn't to force the world and the people in it to be different. Success lies in facing and accepting the truth, growing in harmony with change and opening yourself to learning so that whatever happens you get stronger, bigger, more flexible and more adaptable to change.

Traditional planning concentrates on

the facts—these are usually quantifiable historic data;

the projections—what is deemed possible in the future based on trends in the past; and

the actions—explicit steps to control the future to ensure that the projections can become next year's facts.

In contrast, **strategy in motion** concentrates on

> **reality** as it is happening now—this includes both hard and soft data, for example economic analysis, survey results, dreams of the strategies, personal assessments of the organisation's political reality and mooted changes in legislation. This requires the skill of being able to notice and learn from process;

> **relationships**. If you accept that it is easier to achieve with the cooperation and support of those involved rather than against their wishes, then relationships with others become a key strategic issue. Relationships aren't static rational things and they need to be dealt with in dynamic, human ways. The strategic process becomes a way to enhance our communication and our relationships; and

> **learning**. Change is constant, chaotic and unpredictable, and we really don't know what is going to happen in the future. We can guess. We can also work out what we want and what we think is possible. We can further use every step of the strategic process to learn more about ourselves, more about change, more about leadership, relationship, business and life.

Palmers revisited

What all this means in practice is different for each organisation. In the case of Palmers it meant an ongoing strategic/change process that lasted for a period of several years.

When I sit and think about what I actually did with Palmers it all seems pretty dull, and yet the process was anything but dull.

There was a familiar pattern about the route we travelled and yet each stage held it's own surprises. Every phase involved:

clarification interviews between myself and Ian while he became clear in his mind what he wanted for the next step and why. On these occasions we spent considerable time looking at how we might achieve his objectives, based on our different experiences of leadership and strategic change;

clarification interviews with each of the managers reporting directly to Ian in which I spelt out Ian's desires for the next phase and elicited what they wanted to achieve and why. I also gained feedback as to their progress to date and their preferred method of moving forward;

a period of intense information gathering. The information needed was determined by Ian in conjunction with me, his managers and other sources that seemed relevant to him at the time;

a strategic change retreat of at least 2 days. Each one of these was tailored to meet the business and growth needs of the group. Initially they were highly structured and involved a considerable amount of didactic teaching on my part. Sometimes they were very task focused and at other times we put our attention on the growth needs of the managers, on building relationships within the team or on solving presenting political problems. On every occasion we concentrated simultaneously on personal growth, relationship building, deciding the next stage of focus and growth for the business, and reviewing and building on the organisational change work of each manager;

a period of follow through, again working in the areas of personal development, relationship building, business development and organisational change.

Then we would start the whole process again.

Every time we met, the managers were further advanced than they had been before. Their own growth served as a role model to their people and created the space for their staff to try new ideas and ways of being in safety. At no time did we ever produce a published strategy. We created a living, developing process of strategic growth and change. We produced missions, visions, philosophies and value statements but these often changed as the managers themselves grew. Nothing was fixed, everything was what was appropriate for now and allowed plenty of room for growth while providing people with direction, feedback and support.

Slowly the culture began to change. I worked almost solely with the managers and a group of in-house change agents. What I saw was people coming to life. A spring developed in people's steps, a glint in their eyes. People claimed to have purpose for the first time in years. Relationships improved and people began to take the risk of being real—to say what they really thought, to ask embarrassing questions and suggest new and innovative things. It didn't take long for the business successes to start rolling in. New clients came on board, new technology was put into place and proposed staff cuts became unnecessary because of the increased demand and revenue.

I would be lying if I told you that all of this was easy. Very few people like to change. The managers of Palmers, being human, found it no less easy than others. Whenever we were dealing with tasks they were happy. When we moved onto objectives they were slightly less comfortable but made the transition fairly well. Once we moved into personal development and relationships they felt particularly uncomfortable.   Palmers was a 'nice' organisation. Everybody was agreeable, polite and diplomatic.   In the early days it was impossible to know how people felt, what they wanted or what they thought.   It was the kind of organisation where change would normally be met by a huge report agreeing that change was necessary and then pointing out politely why it couldn't be done.

By using 'I' statements the managers of Palmers were forced out from behind their 'nice guy' exteriors. They were compelled to expose their real fears, reservations, worries and hopes. It would not be an exaggeration to say that they resisted this strongly. They wanted success, they wanted their people to change, they themselves wanted to stay where they had always been hidden—behind strong defences that were too polite and polished to be challenged.

As the defences started to peel away, the managers came up hard against their WOUNDED YOUs. Again they didn't like it. They kicked and fought and demanded that they be allowed to communicate and make decisions as they had before. Then slowly they acknowledged that this new way mightn't be comfortable but it did bring about better results, they did enjoy their work more and they did feel more motivated and inspired than they had in years. Moreover, their relationships had definitely improved; as one manager put it, 'Everybody I know has improved'.

There were times in this, as in most assignments, when I wanted to quit. As the 'change agent', I was the person who had introduced new ways of relating, communicating and decision-making. I was the one who was seen as being the cause of their discomfort. When this happened, the managers hit out. They would refute everything I said, deny my every suggestion and insist that we just 'get on with it'.

At times their anger towards me would be so great that they would pull away and I wouldn't be contacted for some time. Then they would feel ready for the next stage of their growth and back they would come, full of the stories of their successes and looking for more challenge.   My relationship with the managers, like everything else in this process, was dynamic, changing and developing.

My role as I saw it was that of catalyst. The definition of a catalyst is something that facilitates a process but is not consumed by it. The process was there and happening with or without me. My role was to make it easier for change to happen, to help Ian and his managers develop relationships, insights and process that allowed change to occur more rapidly and with greater force.   When this resulted in discomfort for the managers, they rewarded me with the blame. At such times I was pleased to get away and wait until, having recovered from the shock of change, the managers were ready to take responsibility again for their own emotions and actions and move on to the next stage.

To describe the process at Palmers would take a book in itself and would still only be the story of one change process which may or may not be relevant to you and your situation.   What follows, therefore, is a brief description of what lead up to the first strategic change workshop and some of the exercises we used in that and similar workshops, so that you can try them for yourself.

Beginning the process of strategic change

Each strategic change process is begun by the acknowledgement of a need that change is necessary. For this acknowledgement to be successfully translated into action, the leader needs to accept that the need exists and to be prepared to act on it. This can range from a long, drawn-out political battle to the ready admission by an enlightened leader that it's time to try something new.

My first step is to work with the leader to uncover the real issues. I am always anxious to deal with underlying causes rather than presenting symptoms. So often I am asked to deal with a personality clash, or the implementation of a new structure, when really the issue is lack of strategic direction or a hostile and destructive organisational culture.

Once I've agreed with the chief executive as to what the problem really is, I begin my interviews with executives.

I interview each executive personally to see what he or she wants to achieve from the first stage of the strategy process. I seek to ascertain what they see as the key problems and issues. The effects of these interviews are

> that people begin to own the process of strategy and change. It is not the organisation's or the boss's process, it is theirs. They are genuinely being asked for their input because they are considered to be vital and powerful members of the organisation;

> that we begin to create the safety from which people will be able to relax their DEFENDED YOU and gain access to their ESSENTIAL YOU, an important part of the strategic change process; and

> that I gain insight into the presenting problems and opportunities along with preferred methods of the executives to approaching these.

Underlying all this is the philosophy that the optimal strategic and change answers for any organisation can best be found and implemented by the people who work in and run that organisation, and that all they need is assistance in developing the best process to allow them to access their own answers and unleash their own potential and energy.

In the case of Palmers, my interviews with the executives told me that they were used to being told what to do and how to do it. Their expectation was that Ian would call them together and tell them what he wanted and how he wanted it. They would then go away and do what they were told.

My interviews with Ian told me that he wanted his people to grow to the stage where they could do their own research, make their own decisions and follow their own lead. My job was to help Ian bridge the gap. This involved helping his people see that he wasn't the font of all wisdom, didn't know all the answers, wasn't fixed on what was right and how things ought to be. He was, however, clear that he wanted change. He wanted that change to involve technical innovation, customer service, personal development, and an in-built adaptability to change.

I always start and finish my interviews with the chief executive because it is he or she who lays down the political and cultural fibre of the organisation. No matter which way you look at them, organisations are political hierarchies and if we are dealing with reality it is important that this is spelt out along with the expectations and ground rules of the political masters. Ironically, it is these ground rules that provide people with safety. By knowing where the limits are, people are able to decide what level of risk, energy and creative input they are prepared to invest.

In the case of Palmers, my interviews with the executives allowed me to encourage them to review their expectations and begin to open themselves to the possibility that things could be different, even at Palmers.

The next step of the process involved setting very clear objectives as to the desired outcomes of the first stage of the strategic change process. Once these were agreed there was a huge amount of information–gathering to do. The information gathered by Palmers was specific to them and their needs at that time. No two organisations are the same, and what is appropriate information for one is rarely appropriate for another. Some organisations like to use outside consulting firms to provide them with their information, others like to decide for themselves what is important and to gather it in a way that works for them. In my experience most organisations use a whole range of ways of gathering information and having it make sense for them.

Some organisations are information shy and will do whatever they can to avoid surfacing and facing up to the truth. This of course is as dangerous as being bound to historic data. Information matters, it helps us build a picture of current reality so that we can decide how we would like our future to look. It's like selling your house. The price you put on your property is your decision but you base your decision on a whole range of information, including benchmark prices in your area, what the neighbours got when they sold, your predictions about future property values, how much you need to make the sale worth your while, how quickly you want to sell and what the real estate agent advises. You gather the information, mull it over for a while, work out what you want and bingo—you have your price. Strategy isn't too different from that. You need something to start from and after the desire and agreement to start the process, information is a pretty important next step.

One of the forms of information that I encourage people to gain is what their staff like and don't like about working in their organisation. These two simple questions reveal a huge amount of information about what is working and what is not working. The staff are the people on the spot. They are in an excellent position to notice the reality of any organisation. Some leaders refuse to ask their staff. They are frightened of what they might learn. Others claim that their staff wouldn't tell the truth or would only report on unimportant personal things. My experience is that the assessment made by the staff of their own relationship to the employer is an excellent indication as to the strategic strengths and weaknesses of any organisation.

Staff report that the communication is poor, that management doesn't live the message, change their mind often and shun responsibility. They also report that clients' needs are ignored, production times are too long and certain equipment isn't functioning. These are the things that affect the day–to–day life of employees, they are also the things that make or break business success.

The very act of asking the staff is a powerful indication that their point of view matters. In many organisations this is a big change in its own right. I encourage managers at this stage to ensure that staff know that the gathering of this information in no way implies that anything will be done about the information. It is purely information that will be combined with a whole range of other information so that the organisation's leaders can begin the strategy process.

The next stage of this process is a period of at least two days when senior management, equipped with their research, take some time out to make sense of the information to hand. They review their relationships, raise their personal awareness, decide what it is they want for their organisation and themselves and what process they are going to put in train to move towards achieving their goals.

Again I stress that this is a process. What happens on these occasions is less important than how people use the experience that is offered to them. Strategic workshops, lockups and retreats, whatever you like to call them, are a necessary luxury. They are a time of review, renewal and regeneration, an opportunity for leaders individually and as a group to review their priorities—personal and professional— and align their stated options with their inner truths.

This requires time, time for reflection, time for negotiation, time for networking, time to build safety, time to resolve conflicts and time to go beneath the presenting problems to the truth. A group of people can come up with a plausible strategy quickly. They will then find that they have the devil's own job in firstly implementing it and secondly cleaning up the misunderstandings, political wrangles, blocking, stalling and undermining that occurs.

The aim isn't to come up with a 'correct' or laudable strategy. The aim is to come up with a strategy that will work for your organisation at this point. For me that means that the people I have present at any strategic change workshop are the material with which I have to work. It is these people with all their human strengths and weaknesses, who will lead their organisation now and for some time in the future. They may be graced with huge potential and ability, they may not. Either way they are the leaders. The strategy they come up with has to be one they can drive. If they can't make a strategy work it is the wrong one for them. Of key importance to me also is that whatever strategy they devise stretches them, and that they learn and grow from the experiences ahead.

For me this also means that a large amount of time in any strategic change workshop is spent in assisting people to develop learning tools such as ways of increasing their personal, inter-personal and environmental awareness. Strategy isn't about setting a once–and–for–all formula for success, it is about developing relationships that will support and enable you to follow your dreams in a way that ensures that you and your organisation are constantly learning from the experience.

There is no right way to go about strategy when looked at from this perspective. There are no right answers and no tested formulae. There is just a series of minute by minute decisions about what feels right and what might help, based on facing the facts honestly whether they be hard data, emotions, intuitions or subjective assessments.

Coping with changing environments and competing demands

The following exercises are ones that I have used with management groups at strategic change workshops. They allow you to feed in your own information and start to work with it. They also encourage you to move past your DEFENDED YOU into ESSENTIAL YOU as you tap into your intuition and vision. They are a step forward in raising your self and other awareness.

Strategic stakeholder relationships – an exercise

The people with whom we relate in business are called stakeholders. **A stakeholder is a person or group of people who directly or indirectly affect the way that we make and enact decisions.** For you those stakeholders may include customers, competitors, government departments, suppliers, family, shareholders and bank managers. There are many others.

Step 1 List your stakeholders—you may like to categorise them in groups for ease.

Step 2 List all the demands that each stakeholder makes upon you. For example, your customers may demand

- immediate, top quality service
- no mistakes

- that you to listen to and understand them
- to be kept informed

While your boss may demand

- no surprises
- to be kept informed
- loyalty at all times
- top performance
- that you cover his mistakes
- that you read his mind

Your family may demand

- security
- love
- understanding
- that you come home more often
- that you make more money

Step 3 Read out these demands in as demanding a voice as you can. This is a particularly good exercise to do with a management team, with each person in the team taking the part of one stakeholder.

Step 4 Putting your attention inside your body, notice how you feel being bombarded by all these demands. You will notice that stakeholder demands

- are many
- are often contradictory
- range from being caring and concerned through to being downright aggressive

- are complex and often conflicting
- can feel overwhelming and unreasonable
- can feel paralysing
- provide no obvious 'best' course of action
- make it impossible to please everybody and get it right

Follow-up activities

The best way not to feel overpowered by stakeholder demands is for you to take control of the situation, or at least your part of it. There are several ways you might do this.

Listen to your stakeholders and ask for more information with questions such as these: 'Tell me more about what you want.' 'Why is that important to you?' 'How do you see me best helping you?'By doing this, you increase the amount of information you have available to you to make decisions at the same time as letting your stakeholders know that although you mightn't be able to meet all their demands you are very interested in them and their welfare. This will serve to decrease the pressure on you, but be very careful at this stage not to make promises until you have worked out what you want.

Work out what you want—if you can't please everybody you can at least please yourself. The analogy I use is that if you are stuck in a revolving door, and you put your focus on the door, you get dizzy and fall over. Alternatively you panic and try to stop the door, thereby risking your own safety. It is by staying calm and knowing what you want that you get out.

Take the centre of power within yourself and act. In the case of the door, this means shifting your focus from the external problem, deciding to move forward and walking out. In the case of stakeholders, it's deciding what you want and acting on that.

Work out what relationship you will require with each stakeholder to achieve what you want. You can't be all things to all people. You can, however, let people know what you want, what you need and how you would like to relate to them. It is, of course, up to them to decide how they want to relate with you.

Make the necessary changes in yourself and your operations to achieve your desired relationships. The key to this is:

> **you**—your self-awareness
> **your values**—knowing what matters to you
> **your vision**—knowing what you want
> **your openness to learning**—making the necessary changes in yourself to make your dreams come true
> **your commitment to growth**—living in integrity, that is in harmony with yourself, your values and your vision

In times of rapid change these may be the only security and stability that you have. They are also the tools of leadership.

The above exercise helps us to see that we are pretty much pawns in a demanding world unless we take our focus off others and bring our centre of power inward. It acknowledges that we aren't all-seeing and all-knowing nor can we control all the parameters. However we have real power—the power to decide what we want and to work towards getting it.   The following exercises on determining your values and vision are ways of helping you clarify what you want, and working on relationships with some of the people whose involvement and support you may need in getting it.   These exercises are also ways of programming your unconscious to help you prioritise your time, energy and focus in the future.

Determining your values

Your personal values—an exercise

We usually gain clarity about what is important to us when it is in short supply or we may not have it any longer.   The following exercise may shock some people but it is very effective.

Imagine that you have only 6 months to live.   There is nothing that you can do about this—it is a fact.   Now write down how you will fill the next 6 months.   How will you spend your time, who will you spend it with and what will be your priorities?

Most of us spend our time as though it is a limitless resource. We procrastinate, tolerate intolerable situations and generally waste our precious hours.   Yet our time is limited and we don't know how limited it is.   We may be struck down tomorrow or live for another 90 years; either way our time on earth is finite.

The list you made outlines how you would spend your time if you fully realised that it was limited.   You have written down your most valued way of spending your most valuable resource.   Take some time now to write a list of written values.

A written value captures the essence of a way of being that you desire and believe to be important. A typical list might be:

family
peace of mind
love
security
travel

These are your personal values.

Whenever I am working with a corporate management team on their strategic direction I always get them to compile a list of their personal values. By doing this we ensure that their corporate values are consistent with the values by which they personally choose to live. This supports the executives to espouse a set of corporate values and a corporate philosophy with which they can comfortably live rather than one which sounds impressive and businesslike but is at odds with them as individuals.

Corporate values—an exercise

As a management group, combine the personal values ascertained through doing the personal values exercise. Ensure that all of everybody's values are listed. Display this list for the whole group to see.

Now, building from this list, devise a list of corporate values. Corporate values are the ways of being that you believe will create the kind of company you want to work in and lead. Examples of corporate values may be:

integrity
personal development and growth
customer service
balance in all things

The next part of the exercise is to spend as much time as it takes, over as long a period as necessary, to ensure that there is agreement on the definitions of these values. The importance of this is not that you get a technically perfect definition, but the process of decision-making and relationship–building that is involved in talking the definitions through until all members of the team share a common understanding and commitment. This usually takes less time than people think.

This process will be facilitated by the use of 'I' statements as discussed in chapter 3, page 88.

By matching your personal and corporate values you are

- making a step towards aligning your conscious and unconscious being;
- Giving yourself the opportunity to bring more of your unconscious to your awareness by providing a yardstick, for example, 'If I value honesty and I am getting feedback that I am not perceived as honest, what does that tell them about me? About what am I unconscious?';
- Avoiding the need to perjure yourself when you come to work;
- Displaying real integrity.

Your values are your yardstick. These are the things that matter to you. Peace of mind is dependent on your living in accord with your values. Being perceived as an honest, trustworthy and capable leader is dependent on your living in accord with your values. Your values are the flag you wave to the world indicating who you are and what you value.

You will be judged by your values whether you state them or not. You will live by your values whether you state them or not. Real peace of mind and real leadership come from stating clearly the values by which you live. This indicates to you and to everybody else that you know who you are and what drives you. It also encourages others to respect who and what you are. When you state your values, some people may feel they can't live in accord with them. These people will usually, in time, leave your life or work space of their own free will, thus making it easier for you to live in integrity with yourself and those around you.

Visioning

Picture yourself as a circus monocyclist on a high wire suspended across the Big Top. With one hand you are juggling plates, in the other you are balancing a sword on a ball. Now let's suppose that you are a leader, that the plates being juggled are your followers or staff and that the sword on the ball is the external environment. If you concentrate solely on the juggling or on balancing the sword you will fall off and seriously injure, if not kill yourself. If you just sit on your monocycle you will attract a similar fate. The only way to save your life is to pedal. What all good high wire monocyclists know is that at the end of the high wire is a board, and under the board is a ladder. So while you have to juggle, balance and cycle, the aim is to stay alive, to get to the board, go down the ladder and go home.

This is a vision. It is the secret to strategic leadership. It is the art of knowing where you want to go and to keep moving towards it until you get there. Showmanship is keeping the crowd happy by juggling and balancing that sword, leadership is getting to the vision.

Research by Burt Nanus, Warren Bennis and Douglas Mcgregor on leaders who have had a transformational effect on the world tells us that effective leaders have an ability to develop, maintain and communicate a vision. A vision is a view of reality as it could be. Transformational leaders have the ability to experience their vision as if it were real and in the present moment. They can not only see their vision but they can also feel how it is to be part of that vision. They can taste it, hear and touch it in their imagination. Moreover,they can do this so effectively they are able to convince themselves that the vision is real, it just hasn't happened yet.

In terms of focusing energy, visioning is an extremely powerful technique, and all the more so because it involves the whole person. When I envision my future, the first thing I notice is that peace pervades everything. Where I am and what I am achieving are only part of the story. I see myself achieving my goals effortlessly. My primary experience is peacefulness and enjoyment of my family and the people I love.

I have used visioning techniques with a wide range of leaders and have noticed that the very act of visioning improves people's morale and increases their feelings of peace. What is perhaps more surprising is how people have such similar visions of the future to their peers in any organisation, even if they have previously been unable to come to agreement as to how the future might look.

In times of rapid change we really don't know what is going to happen next but we can always be clear about what we want. The following exercises help you do just that.

Envisioning

Before you start, decide at what time in the future you would like to have your vision. I recommend you start with 2 years and then perhaps 5 years. If you are a long–term thinker you may wish to push your vision out to 10, 20 or even 30 years.

Decide whether your vision will be purely work–based or involve elements of home and work. When I am working with new teams of executives in their organisation I usually stick to work, but as a team matures, and in my own envisioning, we include elements of both work and home. This is your life you're working with. It's worth having it work in every aspect—relationship, family, health, work and material success.

If your vision is to include another person or other people, why not invite them to envision with you? I have done this exercise by myself, with my husband, with my children and with my staff and my clients.   I find that by involving others in the exercise you learn what you all want and can align your visions.   This is a wonderful relationship builder as it provides an opportunity for you to discuss your dreams and achievements, ensuring that you grow and move in harmony with each other.   It is counterproductive to envision differently if you want to share the same future.

Envisioning—an exercise

Sit in a comfortable chair or lie on the floor with your knees bent and your feet on the floor.

Cup your hands in your lap.

Close your eyes.

Take a deep breath into the pit of your stomach.

Hold your breath for the count of 10.

Exhale.

Take another two deep breaths into the pit of your stomach, each time holding the breath for the count of 10 before exhaling.

Then concentrate on your breath coming in and going out at its own pace, in and out at its own pace.

In your mind's eye, see yourself at your predetermined time in the future. Try to make yourself aware of the following:

Where are you?
What colours, textures and sounds are around you?
What are you doing?
Who are you with?
What are they wearing?
How old are they?
How have they changed?
What are they saying?
How do you feel?
What tastes are associated with your vision?

Spend as long as you need to really explore your vision—if it seems right, move from situation to situation, from person to person, always ensuring that you experience fully the sights, colours, sounds, physical feelings, emotions and tastes of each situation.

When you have fully experienced your vision, concentrate again on your breath coming in and going out at its own pace.

Then, when you are ready, open your eyes.

If you have done this exercise with another person or in a group, each of you should take some time to write down the elements of your visions, and then discuss your visions looking for commonality. Where did your visions overlap? Where were they compatible? How do you feel about this? What are the implications for the future?

If you did your envisioning alone, you can still write down the elements if you choose. I find it is more effective simply to repeat the exercise regularly, say once a day for about 3 weeks, and to back it up by preparing a storyboard.

Preparing a storyboard—an exercise

Not everybody is good at envisioning. Although practice can make it easier, for some people it will always be difficult. Don't despair. The following technique is just as effective as envisioning and is also a powerful complement to it.

I discovered the storyboard by accident just after I had started up my own business as a management consultant. I had separated from my husband and was in debt and struggling. One morning I looked out the window of my apartment and noticed a smart looking car parked in the street. Not knowing what the car was, I asked a friend who told me that it was a Jaguar. 'I want one of those,' I told him. 'They are very expensive,' was his reply. Some days later I was looking through a magazine and saw a picture of a Jaguar not unlike the one I'd seen in the street. I cut the picture out, pasted it on cardboard and hung it on my bedroom wall. I then forgot the whole thing and went on with my life. About 6 months later, I walked into my accountant's office. My normally conservative accountant advised me that I had made so much money in the past 6 months that I had a tax problem. He advised me to buy a luxury car, 'a Mercedes or a Jaguar'.

It wasn't long before my real Jaguar replaced the one on my wall. I still have that car and every time I look at it I remember that dreams can come true.

I went on to use this technique on many occasions, always

with quick and effective results. When I decided it was time for me to remarry, I sat down with my children, a sheet of cardboard, a whole heap of magazines and scissors and glue. We then cut out the pictures that we felt depicted the kind of family life we wanted to lead. My contribution was some pictures of happy couples enjoying a range of activities, including getting married. About three weeks after that, I met the man who is now my husband. We married 6 months later in his home town of Antibes.

Be warned! This technique is so effective that I recommend you are very careful when you do it. Be very clear about what you want because you have a remarkably good chance of getting it.

How to make a storyboard

1   Decide who you would like to be involved in the making of your storyboard. Do you want to do it alone, with your partner, with your family, with your employees or perhaps with some other group?

2   Decide what the storyboard is to be about—your personal life, your career, your family life, where your business is going over the next 5 years.

3   Collect as many different types of magazines as possible. If you are creating a work–based storyboard you may need to include some trade journals. If you have specific interests then specialist magazines may come in handy. If your range of magazines is limited, don't be disheartened but bestow symbolic meaning on various pictures—for instance, a country scene may symbolise peace and tranquillity, plainly prepared food may represent a simple lifestyle or good

health. Nor are you limited to pictures. You could draw what you want or cut out words.

4   Cut out the pictures and words that you believe represent t h e future you wish to have. Use your imagination. Allow yourself to relax and be a bit self–indulgent. Avoid judging yourself or anyone else. If I could have my Jaguar, why can't your dreams come true?

5   If you are working in a group you may need to discuss the picture and words that you have all chosen. Where pictures are symbolic, make sure that everybody knows what the symbol stands for. When I did mine with my children we actually wrote down the characteristics of the kind of man we would all be happy to accept into our family.

6   Put your pictures on the cardboard, agree upon a layout and paste the pictures and words onto the board. Add any hand drawings and lettering that you wish.

7   Now agree on the best place to display your storyboard. Put it there and be prepared for things to happen.

Commitments

To engage in the above visioning techniques is to send your unconscious some very significant messages.

Firstly, you are telling yourself and others that you deserve to have your life work. Moreover, you are telling yourself that you are a powerful person in your own life. These are first steps on the road to leadership.   What you are in effect doing is taking over the leadership of your own life. You are deciding what you want, and without becoming obsessed by having it and without trying to control the outcomes, you are sending powerful messages to yourself that you can change your view of the world and your situation.

When you do these exercises with others you are opening the door to moving forward together. You are inviting each other, and therefore your relationship, to grow and blossom in directions that you desire mutually.   This is again a positive statement that you matter, that your relationship matters and that you deserve and have the power to affect how you relate.

You are in effect making a commitment to yourself and to each other.   Moreover, you are making a commitment to life. One way of furthering this commitment is to commit to **closing your exits**.

The basis of this technique is that it takes time for change to happen.   Change can also be very uncomfortable and a lot of hard work.   By closing your exits you make a commitment to yourself and to others to stick to your values and vision for a specific period, even if things get sticky, uncomfortable or downright painful. If at the end of the agreed period you don't want to continue, that is fine.

In my experience the benefits of closing your exits is that you really give change a chance. By deciding to stay for a specified period you are really saying that you believe that change is possible and you will give it everything that you have.   You will not sabotage your own attempt to improve your life.

The exits that many of us keep open include suicide, divorce, insanity, drunkenness, total absorption into any hobby or sport, television, hiding behind our children or our work. Exits are the places we escape when being here, in this life, this relationship or this place of work is too uncomfortable. What our exits do is allow us to avoid facing the issues that are getting in the way of our relationships, our lives and our professional success. By keeping our exits open we can go on for years in totally unsatisfactory situations because we know that whenever things get too bad we can retreat into our exits until we cool off, calm down or revive enough to go back to keeping things the way they were.

We then have a perfect excuse to never change, and someone or something to blame for our lives not working. By keeping our exits open we are able to avoid responsibility for our own lives and stay dependant on others.

Harry is a good case in point. Harry was the general manager of a small but growing company. The managing director of the company was a difficult man. He was overbearing, negative, critical and an expert at corporate politics. Harry was frightened of his employer although he was shocked to hear himself admit it. In his imagination Harry saw his managing director as an aging wizard with magical powers. Harry had worked in this unsatisfactory situation for several years, constantly telling himself that he was free to leave at any time and would do so if things got worse. Meanwhile he was able to blame his managing director for anything that went wrong and for Harry's own disappointment that his company had not grown at the rate he would have liked.

The exit Harry had to close was that of leaving. He made a decision to stay for a period of one year, come what may. Realising that he had dedicated one whole year of his life to staying where he was, Harry then faced up to working on his unsatisfactory relationship with his boss. During this time he came to realise that his boss had his own problems, many of them personal and that the managing director's negativity and criticism weren't specific to Harry but an expression of the older man's unhappiness and disillusionment with life.

Realising this, Harry decided to no longer see the managing director as a more powerful person but rather as a human being doing the best he could.   Harry then started to make his own decisions, informing his employer rather than going cap in hand and asking for permission.   To his surprise, the managing director rewarded him with increased support, information and power.   When the managing director slipped back into his old critical ways Harry remembered not to take it personally, offered the older man support and found himself with a close personal friend and ally.

Having decided his company was worth fighting for, Harry faced the problems and solved them.   By closing his exits he learnt some valuable lessons and had his life work for him.

Chapter 5

From Defence To Relationship

Sam is a senior partner in a leading legal practice. His father was a minister of religion and his mother the founder of an international church women's league. As Sam was growing up, being a 'good little boy' was very important. Being seen to do the right things mattered more than just about anything. He worked hard to uphold the family's reputation of 'goodness' and evangelism.

Sam's parents loved him dearly. Their Christian duties, however, meant that they were often distracted or away from home. At such times Sam was left to entertain himself and his younger brother, often feeling lonely and confused.

Sam learnt early that the way to get from his parents the attention he so desperately desired was to do 'good things'. He had a keen natural intelligence which, combined with his willingness to work hard, resulted in his being very successful.

Sam excelled at school, gained honours at the 'right' law school, married a girl from a nice Christian family, worked his way up in a 'good' firm, and was known for the quality of his work. Work Sam did—60, 70, 80 hours a week. He went from success to success. Then his life started to fall apart.

Sam had had affairs on and off for years. 'What people don't see won't hurt them' was his motto. But this time someone did see and that someone told his wife. This information only fuelled suspicions and unhappiness she had entertained for some time. She made a few discreet enquiries and Sam soon found himself faced with a divorce that he didn't want.

Amid the rows and tension at home, his back began to give him trouble. Day after day he was dogged with pain that he could barely endure. It took more and more effort for him to physically get through the day.

As if all that wasn't enough, Sam's mind began to wander. His wonderful, well-tuned, highly trained mind started to play tricks on him. He was disgusted with himself. 'How could he be so unfocused, so undisciplined and so out of control?' Sam had always prided himself on the acuity of his thinking, his level of self-control and his ability to deal objectively with any situation. He wondered what was happening to him and why. He chastised himself for being so weak.

Eventually the combination of pain and distraction led Sam to his local doctor. While waiting in the surgery Sam read an article in a women's magazine. The article was on the increasing rates of stress in women at work. It talked about how rising stress levels are often translated into physical ailments like back trouble, heart and stomach disorders, and how those suffering from stress often lose their ability to concentrate. The article suggested that therapy was a real and justifiable option.

As if by telepathy, that night Sam's wife demanded that they both go to marriage counselling.

Emotions had always been off-limits to Sam. As a child he had believed that the only emotions suitable for good Christian boys were love, compassion and understanding. Little boys left for hours by parents who are out doing good works are rarely filled with love and understanding. If they allowed themselves to feel at all they would notice anger, resentment, fear, despair and hopelessness. So Sam had decided at a young age that emotions were not for him. Therapy being about emotions was equally off-limits. Yet at this point in his life therapy seemed to Sam to be an option. It just might keep him out of the divorce court and save him the embarrassment, financial upheaval and emotional strain of a failed marriage. So Sam agreed to his wife's request and they began to see a marriage counsellor.

Sam remembers this as the beginning of the rest of his life. As he and his wife worked through their problems together, he began to see how many of the problems in their marriage had been caused by his inability to feel, and therefore to respect the feelings of others. Moreover, as Sam began to discover some of his emotions, he found that there was much more to life than his narrow 'good boy' existence. He began to discover within himself creativity, fun and joy that he had never known before. His life took on a whole new dimension. His marriage was not only saved but improved dramatically. Moreover, he found that while working substantially fewer hours each week, the quality of his relationships with both his staff and clients improved. This translated into an increase of revenue flowing into the practice and a raising of status for Sam with his partners.

Sam now considers he was extremely lucky that his repressed emotions caused him so many problems and forced him to change. Sam's life before the crises had been full but of poor quality. He had had little intimacy, very little real enjoyment and was a slave to his 'old brain' fears and neuroses. It was only when things went completely off the rails that he was prepared to notice that his life wasn't working and began to accept that he had problems. Like an alcoholic, he had had problems all the time. It was only when he was prepared to admit it that he could do something constructive about the situation.

The role of emotions

Our emotions will press us towards our own good health every time. They will tell us when there is work to be done on old emotional problems and on correcting existing situations. Our emotions are the first warning sign when things are not going well. They will tell us when our rights are being denied, when we are overstressed and when we need to take some time out to think. Our emotions will tell us when it's time to change, time to take a holiday and time to work on improving our relationships. Our emotions will tell us when something or someone in our environment is dangerous and will give us advanced warning of most impending change.

It's up to us to hear what our emotions have to say. To do this we need to spend time getting to know, understand and respect these friendly and much maligned messengers.

Emotions at work

Emotions are a vital part in any human change process. They underlie all our relationships and are an essential part of being human.Most workplaces, however, have been designed so as to outlaw emotions. Written on many office and workshop walls in invisible ink are the words 'NO EMOTIONS ALLOWED'. Basic management theory tells us that emotion is subjective and therefore has no place in the rational world of business and government. The answer we have been led to believe and trained to execute is to leave our feeling selves at home. Of course, a quick look around any place of work soon reveals that emotions are *not* left at home. Like any outlaw, they simply go into hiding and pop up at times when they are least expected and most dangerous. Like alcohol during prohibition, outlawed emotions simply go underground where they thrive beyond the control of our awareness. Banning emotions at work just means that they are less controllable, more unpredictable and a far greater threat to public and personal well-being. When it comes to emotions, it is what you can't see and don't know about that can hurt you the most. Banning emotions at work merely pushes us further into our DEFENDED YOU where we operate out of our unconscious defences. This ensures that our organisations are even less rational than they would otherwise be.

Johnathon's Story

Johnathon had heard through contacts that I was able to help people who had problems that arose out of the intersection of business strategy and human relationships. He wanted to know if I could help him.

Johnathon was a highly successful entrepreneur. He had built from scratch a group of companies valued at some $20 million which he was in the process of selling to a multinational buyer. The sale was being delayed by a revolt in his own boardroom. The minority shareholders had banded together to divest Johnathon of his power in order to capitalise their own gain from the sale. Johnathon found this particularly painful as his directors were all past employees who he had brought to Board status as a recognition of their service and past loyalty. He couldn't understand why people he had helped to such an extent were so keen to win at his expense.

As if his troubles at this time weren't enough, Johnathon was recovering from the break-up of his marriage and a recent car accident which jeopardised the full use of his left arm.

Couldn't I call the Board members together, get everybody to see reason and come up with an equitable win-win solution?

I explained to Johnathon that I could only work with people who wanted to change. The only person who wanted Johnathon's Board to be different was Johnathon. If he could convince the other directors to seek help I was happy to oblige, otherwise there was little I could do.

Still Johnathon wanted answers. Why was his Board behaving this way? What had gone wrong? What could he now do?

As we talked it became evident that one of the Board members was a woman with whom Johnathon had had a long-standing affair. His problems had started when he ended the relationship in an attempt to save his marriage. Fuelled by bitterness and despair, his rejected lover had rallied the other Board members around her and convinced them that Johnathon was about to leave the country with their share of the sale proceeds. They believed her because Johnathon had such a manipulative management style that he had lost their trust.

Johnathon had a quick, sharp mind and an impeccable sense for business. He had little difficulty working out what people needed to do to make things work and then cleverly beguiled them into adopting his preferred behaviour. He was invariably right and his employees soon learnt that playing the game Johnathon's way lead to personal success and favours from the boss. He attributed his company's growth to his keen insight and great skill in manipulation.

What these talents had failed to bring Johnathon was the trust, loyalty or caring of the people around him. He was in jeopardy of losing what he had achieved because he had never learnt how to lead in a way that allowed people to be true to themselves, to contribute from their own essence and to grow and learn as people. He had created a company worth millions based on the foundation of very unstable relationships. When change came and the company was shaken, the foundations fell and were in danger of taking Johnathon down with them.

When he arrived, Johnathon's whole focus was on getting the others in his life to change. The more we talked, the more he began to see that it was his insistence on forcing others to be his way that had caused his problems in the first place. By manipulating those around him, Johnathon had destroyed the relationships that he needed for success. While he was winning, he was safe. Now he was vulnerable and those around, fuelled by years of resentment, were getting back at him, and it was hurting. Johnathon could go on playing the old games or he could learn. His learning would probably be too late to help him rescue these relationships, and this failure would cost him dearly. He was, however, young enough, smart enough and had enough energy to start again.

Johnathon had used his concentration on business to avoid growing and learning as a person. He had lost at his own game through failing to notice and work on his own weaknesses.

Relationships

Relationships are vital to achieving Peaceful Chaos. They will not only allow you to achieve durable strategic success but will provide you with the personal support and growth you need to enjoy your life in all its aspects. Relationships bring us

>personal fulfilment and support
>joy
>love
>learning
>information

companionship
broadened perspective
achievement of goals and vision
support—both practical and emotional

What we get from our relationships is a direct result of what we bring with us to them. It's not that the other person's contribution to the relationship is not important, it is just that the only parts of our relationships over which we have any control at all are our attitudes, our skills, our personal needs and our qualities. The only part of our relationships that we can experience and affect is *our* part.

In public life we tend to see relationships as instrumental. We believe that we have to cultivate and nurture relationships simply in order to meet our objectives. Most courses on relationship for managers teach techniques to help you influence other people so that they will respond to you in the way that helps you. Some of the more enlightened courses teach win–win ways of doing this to ensure that the other person gets enough of their needs met to happily give you what you want.

That relationships and people are valuable seems to most managers to be not work related and therefore not appropriate for leadership. They see love, caring and mutual enjoyment as subjective, out-of-work concepts—definitely not strategic or practical.

Management is based on the premise that people are useful in so far as they perform a set of tasks in a way that leads to attainment of the goals of the manager. People's value is measured in how they can contribute to the leader's goal rather than as a function of the intrinsic value as human beings.

I remember the scepticism of my personal assistant when I expounded this philosophy to her. A sensible, practical person, she was sure that I was crazy. She knew that you couldn't pay people just to be themselves; that would lead to bankruptcy. Of course she is right—if people don't contribute to the success of the business you can't afford to pay them. The more they contribute, the more money is available for salaries. This reality needs to be acknowledged and its natural consequences fed back to people through well-designed reward systems. This is, however, no reason why our common need to make our organisations work should result in a devaluing of our relationships with each other as human beings.

People are people and as such are valuable. Your appreciating people in the fullness of who they are enriches them, you and your relationship together. You can respect each other, acknowledge and value each other's differences and care for each other on an emotional level, even at work. This supports your working together to achieve objectives. Of course, there will be occasions when you will tread on each other's toes, do things the other person doesn't like, fail to meet commitments or not perform to standard. These things are only human. What makes or breaks relationships is how you respond to and treat each other on such occasions, how you communicate and how available you are to contact each other emotionally.

Part of my assistant's duties are to manage my household so that I don't have to worry about the day-to-day practicalities of housing, feeding and taking care of a family. For some time Liska was happy to perform these duties and then she found that we were making her job too hard by being messy and inconsiderate. She approached me about doing less 'housework'. I care deeply about Liska. I like her and I like having her in my life. I listened to her complaints and they made sense to me. I then told her how much she mattered to me, how I liked working with her and didn't want her to find her job arduous. I also explained that her job was 'to manage' the household, not to support irresponsible behaviour on the part of me and my family. We looked at the difference between managing and doing, discussed what behaviours we all needed to change and then wrote up a list of rules that Liska felt was fair. That evening we had a family meeting and discussed the issue and the rules. Everybody accepted that the requested changes were reasonable and they were put into place.

Some days later Liska mentioned that my telling her how much I valued her was the first occasion in her life when anyone had expressed so deep a concern for her as a human being. She acknowledged that she now realised that if you value those around you, you build their loyalty, commitment and desire to be of service.

The not–for–profit sector understands this philosophy better than just about anyone. Across the world, millions of people work hard and well for nothing or for much less than they deserve because they feel valued as a human being. They literally work for love. What a pity those in the areas of government and business have lost the ability to love those with whom they work. It would enrich the lives of everybody and raise productivity dramatically.

Unfortunately most relationships between managers and their staff could best be described as a power struggle. The manager attempts to get people to conform to prescribed roles and work towards a set of objectives that have little intrinsic value to the worker and generally serve to alienate people from themselves and from those around them. In this alienated state, the most usual outcome is friction, resentment, dissatisfaction, competition and contempt. Because it is politically dangerous to acknowledge or express any of these emotions, they are suppressed. They fester out of sight and conscious awareness only to flare up covertly as resistance, blocking or undermining, or overtly as industrial action, litigation or challenges to power.

WOUNDED YOU

In the face of all this we 'know' that the only safe way to behave in organisations is to develop and hide behind our DEFENDED YOU. Who would be fool enough to risk exposing our vulnerable emotional selves to the war zones that exist in most workplaces? So we engage in empire building, withholding of the truth, emotional shutdown, denial and the whole gamut of political games that are the accepted norm in public life. We meet the battle with all guns loaded and then wonder why at the end of the day we are so tired, depleted and have so little peace.

The latest trend of 'empowerment' is largely aimed at diffusing this management/worker tussle by pushing power down the line, introducing team–based worker participation and by removing layers of management. The hope is that people will be able to relate in more cooperative and less combative ways.

Unfortunately, these well–intentioned moves often ignore the realities of organisational life and fail completely to deal with people's defences or emotions. Organisations are power hierarchies in which some people have more say, more control over resources and more freedom than others. People are complex creatures who are slow to change.

All of this makes relationships in organisations very difficult indeed, and yet without functioning relationships organisations can and do grind to a halt.

Change

The problem is that no one wants to take the first step to do things differently. Everybody is frightened that if they lower their barriers and reveal their human vulnerability they will pay too dearly. In fact, because this fear stems largely from the 'old brain' which sees everything in terms of life and death, our deep unconscious fear is that we will be annihilated. So we play a game in which the best and most cleverly defended people appear to win. By shielding their vulnerability, they climb to the top where they work long and hard to stay.

The cost of working this way is high.   We jeopardise ourselves, our emotional well-being, our relationships and our health. We also greatly limit the possibilities that come from having people working together in a supportive way, drawing on the energy, creativity and insight that lies in their ESSENTIAL YOU.

Unfortunately, most of us can't even visualise it being different. Virginia Satir, the mother of family therapy, tells us that 95 per cent of families are dysfunctional.   As Dr Charles L. Whitfield defines it in *A Gift to Yourself*, a dysfunctional family is one that is not a safe place for the 'psychological and spiritual well-being and growth of each of its members'. This means that a 'normal' family in our society is not a healthy family. As a society we grow up thinking that behaviours that are dysfunctional are normal. We take this thinking with us to work where it is reinforced. We think that to feel and express our emotions is political suicide, to show our vulnerability is stupidity and to think of people as anything other than 'human resources' just isn't business.

The only way to change is to take a big leap into the unknown, to risk believing that there has to be a better way than this and to go out and find it. People usually do this when they are faced with personal disasters like Sam or Johnathon, or like Peter in chapter 3, when they want more out of life, work and success than they are currently getting.

These are the lucky ones. They have the impetus to take a risk that most people are too scared to entertain. Their level of discomfort with the status quo is sufficiently high to look for an alternative.

An alternative

My experience tells me that leaders want practical answers that are clearly visible and quick to implement. The only alternative that I know appears to be none of these things. It's not that my suggested alternative won't result in practical, visible results, it's just that the path to the outcome is through the diffuse and nebulous mechanisms of human thought and emotion. The process is inherently hard to see, and we are remarkably unskilled at noticing even that which is discernible. Moreover, our level of personal consciousness is so low that most of us can't even see the problem. To make the shift to being aware of the problem and the process that leads to its remedy, we have to move way outside our comfort zones into areas we can't even envisage at the moment. It's like the explorers of time past. They took off on their voyages totally unaware of what they might find or even how they might get to their goal. Many had to pass through uncharted waters and face the fear that if the world were flat they might just fall off the edge and never come back. Like the explorers, the only way to find out is to make the journey.

The journey to which I refer is, of course, the path to Peaceful Chaos. As we have seen this involves:

>raising your awareness of your DEFENDED YOU and noticing how and when you defend;

>contacting your WOUNDED YOU and learning to nurture yourself back to emotional wholeness so that you can listen to and learn from your emotions;

> building up your ESSENTIAL YOU so that it can
> replace your need for heavy defences by building your
> strength, talents and energy from within.

In essence this means shifting your attention from controlling the
external environment to raising your awareness of yourself and how
you experience and relate to the world around you.   It means
changing your intention from being right and winning to an intention
to learn not only about the environment and the people in it but
about yourself.   It also means developing a new range of practices
and skills that allow you to increase your awareness, build your
relationships and learn more fully from every experience.

Initially people find most of these things rather scary.   They
are sure that in concentrating on their own experience, in feeling
their own feelings and in letting down their defences they are
opening themselves to danger—which they are. When we begin to
feel,   we   notice   pain,   despair,   sadness,   remorse,   guilt   and
hopelessness, along with joy, love, peace, happiness and inspiration.
You can't have one without the other.   Moreover, as we begin to
lower our DEFENDED YOU we will be more affected by bullying,
betrayal and coercive behaviour that is a common part of public life.

All of this is a blessing.   When you begin to really feel what
it is like to be bullied, betrayed and coerced you become incredibly
motivated to change the situation.   You find yourself impelled to
renegotiate relationships, change your way of working and find more
palatable alternatives.   Deadening your emotions so as not to feel
pain doesn't stop people hurting you. It just encourages you to
repress such hurt and increase your lack of consciousness. This
makes as much sense as anaesthetising the skin so that you won't
feel the pain of putting your hand in the fire.   Feeling emotional
pain helps you make rational decisions about putting yourself at
risk—it puts you more in touch with both your environment and

yourself. There is no faster road to success in times of rapid change than the ability to be fully emotionally, mentally and spiritually aware and to be open to the learning that this awareness affords. Isn't it a delight that this is also the path to personal well–being, health and inner peace?

Safe people

Moving towards Peaceful Chaos is a bit like learning to ride a bicycle. When you start you're a bit shaky and you need somewhere safe to practise so that should you topple over, you don't get so badly hurt that you can never ride again. As your skill increases, you move from a back paddock or footpath to riding on back roads, and then when you are very good, onto the highway. Riding a bike at any time involves a risk. Some places are, however, inherently more risky than others. It makes sense to practise where you are the most safe until you are sufficiently skilled to provide for your own safety, make your own judgements and ride where you choose.

The greatest help to get you started on the road to Peaceful Chaos is to find a safe person. A safe person is someone who can create around them enough safety for you to practise being human, vulnerable, present and aware. A safe person does this simply by being themselves.

They can accept their own emotions, truth and vulnerability sufficiently to create safety for others to follow suit. A safe person can listen and hear what you have to say without their own repressed emotions and illusions getting in the way. A safe person cares for the real individual, not for the image or the charade. A safe person is non–judgemental, clear and loyal. They set their limits. You know where you stand with a safe person.

There are very few safe people in public life. In fact with only 5 per cent of families supporting psychologically and spiritually healthy people, there aren't a lot of safe people anywhere. But it is safe people who can show us another way.

Safe people, by allowing us to be ourselves, provide us with the perfect environment for learning and growth. They role model that being different is possible. Safe people don't look any different from anyone else but they feel very different to be around. You just feel better in the company of a safe person. You can relax, be yourself, let down your barriers and know you are safe.

With safe people you feel supported to experience whatever emotions are current for you. You can be as emotionally alive as you are capable of being. In the absence of judgement you feel safe enough to start to look at your own weaknesses, your blind spots, your own pain and areas of vulnerability. You have someone to help you make sense of what you find from your new learning. With a safe person you can face the truth knowing that you won't be punished or rejected and can use what you find to learn and grow.

With a safe person you can try new experiences and know that you will be accepted even if you fail.

A safe person won't relieve you of your responsibility for yourself. So with a safe person you can learn to increasingly own your new learning.

When leaders are safe people, they are sufficiently human to allow other people to be human, to face reality, to learn and to grow. They promote creative problem–solving, dynamic teamwork, good communication and strategic being. They are rare. It takes courage, persistence, commitment and strength to be a safe leader. It takes a willingness to show the way by being the first to deal with your emotions, your pain, your failings and your blind spots.

Safe people are the best teachers because they support you to find your own path. The road to Peaceful Chaos is the road to becoming a safe leader. This is such a rare path that you will need to find role models and support to inspire and sustain you on the journey.

At this stage I am struck by the difficulty of putting into words a process that has to be experienced to be understood. Each step in itself means little. I can not present you with a set of tools which if applied will lead to the desired result. It just isn't that easy. A set of tools would more likely be adopted by and built into our DEFENDED YOU in such a way as to make us more cleverly defended. What works is not following a formula for change but engaging in a process of change. Each part of that process is extremely simple and, yet because it is so different from what we have done in the past and because our consciousness is so low at the beginning, we need constant reinforcement, constant feedback and constant challenge to succeed.

What I can offer you is a series of exercises that will help you to experience some of the concepts and changes to which I allude. I can also urge you find yourself a safe person with whom to practise your new skills and awareness. The key to change is less about learning a load of skills than it is about committing to notice the process of life in which you are engaged, having the courage to go where you have never been before and creating the opportunity to experience how it is to relate in safety.

Raising Awareness

I developed the following exercise for the executive team of a major bank. The exercise is aimed at helping people put into practice and internalise the concepts of heightened personal awareness and responsibility as applied to a strategic work–based issue. The exercise will not only help you raise your awareness, it will also increase your feelings of peace and inner power. You will find that you feel more in control and less stressed by approaching any issue along these lines.

Reflecting on Process

Before going into a meeting, negotiation or discussion, take the time to go through the following process.

1   Be honest with yourself about what you really want to achieve. Ask yourself:

- What is my emotional involvement in this issue?
- What would I like to achieve?
- How can I approach this issue in a way that will improve the quality of my working life and peace of mind?
- What can I learn about myself from my present response to this issue?
- What can I learn about myself from observing my behaviour during the process?

2   Be prepared to suspend existing preconceptions about

- the way things are;
- the way things should be;
- the way other people think, feel and act;
- the way other people should think, feel and act.

3   Open to the possible in the following ways:

- Start looking at things the way they really are,
  not the way you think they are or should be.
- Collect appropriate information.
- Take in the signals, signs and happenstances
  without judgement.
- Listen, really listen to what people have to say.
- Inquire, really inquire, with empathy and without
  judgement, how it is for others and what they hope
  to achieve.

4   Believe in yourself and take responsibility.

- The only person who is responsible for your success
  or failure is you. The only person who has real
  power over you is you.
- The only person you can change is you. Nobody can
  force you to do anything.
- You have no control over other people, events or
  contingencies, yet you have great influence and are
  always responsible for the outcomes that affect you
- Nobody is more powerful than the person who
  believes they can make a difference and who is
  prepared to take responsibility for everything that
  happens to them.

Therefore ask yourself:

- How much of the presenting problem is me?
- How much of it have I created, maintained
  and nurtured?

- Do I even want to address the issue/s?
  Why? Why not?
- Whose problem is it?
- How much am I part of the solution?

5   Get your house in order.

- What is it about the way that I think, feel and act that will contribute to my achieving my desired outcomes whilst maintaining my peace of mind?
- Is there anything that I currently think, feel or do that is counterproductive to my achieving outward success and inner peace?

6   Reassess what you really want.

Grounding

All we can ever know is our own perception of reality: if we miss this we miss life altogether. Yet so many of us are focused on where we are going, where we have been and what is happening for other people that we simply don't have the skills to notice the process of our own life and experience. It is in our own process that the learning that will take us into Peaceful Chaos lies. The following exercise helps us to be sufficiently present to notice our own experience. It is a first step in becoming our own teachers.

Exercise in grounding

Sit in a comfortable chair with your feet on the floor. If you are wearing high–heeled shoes take them off.

Concentrate on your breath coming in and going out at its own pace. Then begin to notice.

Notice what you can hear. Birds? Electrical equipment? A plane flying overhead? A tap dripping? The lapping of waves or the gurgle of a river? Traffic? Voices? Building work? Notice what you can sense. Your feet in your shoes? Your bottom on the chair? A breeze across your skin? Warmth from a fire?

Notice what you can taste. Something bitter? Something sweet? Afternoon tea?

Notice what you can smell. Babies? Cleaning fluid? A human smell? Smoke? Perfume? Air–freshener? Flowers?

Notice what you can see. A smiling face? A book? A yellow flower? A tree just out the window?

Now notice how you feel. Relaxed? Happy? At peace? Worried? Sad? Depressed? Anxious?

The idea is to just notice. Not to judge or analyse or try to change anything, just notice. We are so bad at noticing, you may find this exercise hard and you may need a lot of practice. All you are doing is practising being you, here on this planet and aware of who you are and where you are. Isn't it interesting that we have to learn to do this? Yet by not being present we are cutting out the reality of life, and thus making our decisions and basing our actions on what should be, might be, could be and ought to be rather than on what is.

Keeping a journal

Another way of slowing down enough to notice is to keep a journal. A journal is a personal friend you can speak to once a day and tell what is happening for you. I have found that just by writing in my journal my problems seem to solve themselves. With the writing of my experiences come insights, inspirations and creative flashes that I would otherwise have completely missed.

I find it fascinating that we spend so much time and money seeking professional advice on things to which we know the answers. Managers laugh that they pay consultants large amounts of money to 'borrow your watch and tell you the time'. 'All the consultants did,' complain the managers, 'was tell us what we already knew.' The reason that such consultants are paid so highly is that they do for managers what managers are loath to do for themselves and that is listen to the manager's own wisdom. Of course, the payment to the consultant is also for having him or her take responsibility for the outcome. Very few people have the courage to listen to their own truths and back up their own judgements.

A journal is like your own free consultant, someone who will tell you what you already know—they'll even do it in writing. The chief difference between a journal and most consultants is that you are left with the responsibility for your own thoughts, feelings and actions. You are also left with a lot of insight into how you are going and why and what you might do next. You will also be left with a growing sense of wholeness, of peace and a growing affection for and understanding of yourself.

The above exercises may well put you in touch with emotions with which you are uncomfortable. These exercises will help you to work constructively with those emotions and use them to learn and grow.

Contacting WOUNDED YOU

Body-mind

When you become aware of an emotion you wish to explore, sit quietly and put your attention on your body. Notice how the emotion you are exploring feels within your body. Where is it situated? How big is it? What flavour does it have? Just let your awareness settle within the emotion and feel it fully.

Now ask your body to remember the earliest time you can recall experiencing this feeling. Where were you? Who were you with? What were you doing? What triggered the emotion? Feel how it was to be you at that time, experiencing this emotion. Notice what, if any, decisions you made at this time about how you would relate to life. Experience how you felt whilst making those decisions.

Explore what you have learnt. Were you able to see any patterns associated with this emotion? Are these patterns serving you? Are the decisions you made still relevant? Would you like to remake them?

The above technique takes time and practice to develop its full benefits. The earlier we can remember back, the closer to our driving patterns we become. I have found that for most executives it takes months, sometimes years, of practice before they can get back to very early memories. The following exercise is a little more contrived but it serves as a trigger for very early experiences. Some people may find the experiences they uncover through doing this exercise very painful and I recommend that you do it in the presence of someone you trust so that they can support you if you discover things about yourself and your past you find painful.

Revisiting the past

When you notice an emotion you would like to explore, put your awareness within your body and notice where in your body you store the emotion. Spend some time exploring the emotion.

Now, in your imagination, travel back to your earliest childhood home. See yourself as a very young child and experience your home as you did when you were a child. Walk from room to room and notice how they look, smell and feel. Let the people you lived with in this house come into your picture and experience them as you did at this age.

Now let your awareness return to your initial emotion. When do you remember first feeling this emotion in your earliest childhood home? Know that you are totally safe and that nothing or nobody is going to hurt you. Notice what was happening when you first experienced this emotion. Notice who was involved and how you and they related. Notice what decisions you made. Now in your imagination, knowing that you are completely safe, talk to your parents, caregivers, brothers or sisters and tell them anything that you feel would free you to be more fully yourself. Trust that they will welcome your comments and support you in your learning and growth.

When you are ready, return to this time and space and talk your experience through with a safe person, just noticing what you learnt, and remaking any decisions you see fit.

Building up your ESSENTIAL YOU

Strategic thinking time

One of the ways we avoid feeling and being aware is that we keep ourselves so busy we don't have a second for ourselves. We create a thousand diversions all of which keep our mind fully occupied. We convince ourselves that if we let go of any of the 'busi–work' in which we engage there would be major problems. We con ourselves into believing that we are indispensable, that 'If you want something done well you have to do it yourself', and we set ourselves and others unrealistic levels of perfection. As doing the impossible takes a little longer, we are always flat out.

All of this leaves us depleted, stressed and flustered. It also helps us to feel important, needed, in control and self–sacrificing. When we overstretch ourselves we undermine our ability to think and to feel. We end up like the dog chasing cars. We might be achieving our goals, but at what price and for what ultimate benefit?

What we fail to realise is that we behave in this crazy way for the very good reason that it avoids having to think about how we feel, face reality and do something meaningful about it. Our 'business' is often an ongoing self–con to avoid having to take responsibility for our lives. By being 'too busy' we can avoid the self–awareness and growth necessary for intimate relationships, a deep sense of inner peace and the ability to work strategically towards meaningful goals.

I have witnessed this creative avoidance in myself and my clients so often now that I know how endemic it is to our society. Some of us have even elevated it to an art form. Just about every management book I have read is full of 'to do' lists—I get tired just reading them. We have created filofaxes and whole computer systems to support our addiction to 'busi-ness'. We complain about it and go to time management courses, ignoring the fact that we created our 'busi-ness' for some excellent, if unconscious and self-destructive, reasons.

There is only one way to stop this behaviour and that is to stop doing it. That's right, you just don't do it any more.

When you notice that you are rushing around like a headless chook, when you hear yourself take on yet another task that could easily be done by someone else, when you hear yourself say, 'I'll do it or it will never get done,' stop and take notice.   It might be strategic thinking time.

Strategic thinking time is a prerequisite for leadership.   It is something that you do to improve your performance as a leader. You do it for the people you lead, for your customers, for the family and for the shareholders.   If you need to you can even be self-sacrificing about it.   I tell you this because people have a tendency to feel guilty about strategic thinking time.   They reason that anything that feels this good can't be helpful, but let me assure you that it is.

When you notice that you are really creating hurly burly, when you hit yet another crisis, when you are losing all the arguments you've been having with yourself—you are really of very little use to anyone. You may be going through the motions but it is questionable how much you are achieving or even if they are the right motions. So this is when you

- go for a walk
- call your partner and go out to lunch
- pick up the kids and go to the park
- play golf
- spend time seeking support from someone you trust
- go home and take a shower

- have a massage
- have a pedicure
- go for a swim
- sit under a tree and contemplate the flowers.

Let me assure you that by behaving this way you are saving your employer's/shareholders'/clients' money. You are saving your sanity and the sanity of those with whom you work. You are also creating enough space for you to be present. It is only when you are present that you can notice how you are thinking, feeling and acting. It is only when you are present that you start behaving responsibly. It is only when you are present that you can think strategically.

I schedule strategic thinking time into my diary on a regular basis because I have learnt that without peace, clarity and awareness I underperform, underachieve and stop enjoying being who I am and enjoying doing what I am doing.

Strategic thinking time gives me an opportunity to slow down long enough to catch up with myself, and puts me in a position to make informed, rational decisions.

Feeling the essence

I devised the following exercise for a client who was suffering from cancer. He wanted me to create a healing tape for him. I am unsure whether the exercise helped him with his cancer but it did, and continues to do, *me* a power of good. I do the exercise two or three times a day with great benefit.

Either follow the steps of the relaxation exercise on page 62, chapter 2.

OR sit with your feet on the floor, without high–heeled shoes, hands cupped in your lap and eyes closed.Take three deep breathes into the pit of your stomach, holding each breath for the count of 10 before exhaling. Then concentrate on your breath coming in and going out at its own pace.

Each time you breathe in, picture a golden light entering your body. This is a healing light that brings with it peace, love, joy and health.

Every time you breathe out, notice that the breath takes with it any tension, worry, stress or illness that you may be feeling.

If you have any physical illness, allow the light to circulate the affected area of your body, cleansing and healing that area.

The outbreaths remove any disease, along with the anxiety and concern that attaches to the disease.

Continue experiencing the value of the healing light coming in and the diseased thoughts and energies going out.

Then notice around you a strong yellow light that connects and strengthens the light within you. Know that the light within you is yours and is always available to you. The light outside you is also available whenever you ask for it and will strengthen your inner light on call.

Accept that with the strength of the light available to you, you are never alone or unprotected and you have nothing to fear. Wherever you go and whatever you do you will be safe. You are more than just a physical body: as a body of light, you are whole and healed, happy and at peace. You have available to you an infinite source of energy, creativity, peace and joy. You need never fear, you are always protected.

Experience the joy, health, peace, safety and happiness of the light for as long as you wish. Then concentrate on your breath coming in and going out at its own pace. When you are ready, open your eyes.

Chapter 6

Helping Others To Change

Not long into any management change process people are beginning to feel less need to defend, more comfortable with their emotions and are starting to enjoy the benefits of growing intuition, clarity, creativity and improved relationships. Then the cry goes up: 'We want to take this to our people.' 'Our people' usually number in the thousands. I know that the change process is slow, time intensive and simply doesn't work without the presence of a 'safe person'. I also know that people lower down in an organisation are less likely to risk change if they haven't seen changes in their leaders.

I have always operated on the philosophy that as managers themselves become safe people change in the ranks below will happen as a matter of course. This takes time and managers get impatient so we need to work on many fronts. The danger in working down the line too quickly is that managers will use the excuse of helping others change to abandon their own growth process. It takes years for people to shift their focus from familiar, external issues to the less comfortable and more challenging dynamics of personal and interpersonal learning.

Yet there is no more effective way of changing an organisation than the leaders of that organisation thinking and acting differently. On the next page are the key ways that leaders can bring about real change in the people around them.

- role—modelling change
- becoming a safe person
- creating space for change to happen
- catalysing change

Role—modelling change

Evan was a busy production manager in a large manufacturing company. He found that his job required him to work long hours and left him depleted at the end of the day. His wife and two children complained about the situation but Evan explained that he simply had more to do than time in which to do it. As he was the breadwinner, Evan pointed out, the family would need to find a way around the problem. He didn't like feeling tired at the end of every day and hated the unhappiness he saw in his family. He regretted what was happening to his relationships. He could, however, see no end to the constant demands of his employment.

Evan's wife, Liz, had trained as a social worker. She had stopped working while the children were small. When her youngest child entered school Liz became impatient to return to her profession. Evan convinced Liz, however, that he needed her at home to support him and the family, that with him working so hard she was a necessary back—up to the family's lifestyle. Initially, Liz accepted his arguments, but became more and more unhappy. Evan worked harder and harder and things generally got worse. Then one day Liz saw a social work position advertised in the local paper. On impulse she applied, and within two weeks had been asked when she could start. Relationships in Evan's household became particularly strained as Liz, against all Evan's protests, accepted the job offer and began work.

The situation went from bad to worse when Liz started demanding that, since she too was now working, Evan needed to take more responsibility at home. She organised a sharing of the tasks between herself, the children and Evan and refused to do more than her share. She avoided mopping up after anyone who didn't fulfil their responsibilities, and even took time out to walk on the beach and visit friends. Evan got angrier and angrier. This wasn't the way things were meant to work at all.

It was about this time that I began to work with the management team of which Evan was a member. A large part of our work was about letting go the pretence of control over the situations and the people around us. Evan began to sort out where his true responsibilities lay. He set priorities for himself clearly and was thus able to concentrate on the things that mattered most and for which he was responsible.

Extraneous matter he delegated to his subordinate. As Evan started to invest less energy in trying to control the way the people around him acted and thought, he found that his subordinates grew into their responsibilities and provided him with their ideas, skills and innate abilities in a way that they hadn't before.

Miraculously, Evan didn't need to invest such long hours in his work. He was able to get home earlier, spend more time with his family and even began to enjoy playing 'house husband' out of hours. His relationship with his wife improved enormously. He started to relax and move increasingly into his ESSENTIAL YOU.

Evan's wife had done him a great service. Her change had provided a huge incentive for Evan to look for new ways of operating. All her nagging, complaining and whingeing had got her nothing but unhappiness. What had worked was being different herself. Moreover, her strength of resolve and determination to delegate to Evan and the children, despite their active efforts to stop her, had provided Evan with a wonderful role model that delegation, even in unfavourable conditions, is possible. Through her actions Evan's wife had shown him that successful change is not necessarily comfortable nor welcomed by those around you.   Change takes courage, determination and a strong belief that you and your needs are worth asserting.   To help others change we need to set our limits clearly at the same time as staying emotionally open to those affected by our change.   This can be extremely challenging as people faced with change in someone close to them often behave in rather unpleasant and unlovable ways.

When I pointed this out to Evan, he laughed—he hadn't seen things that way.   Evan went on to display in his own leadership style the same amount of courage, determination and love demonstrated by his wife.

We all know that actions speak louder than words, but it's so much easier to talk about change than to show the world we mean business.

Communication

Most organisations claim to have a communication problem and yet to my mind communication in most organisations is just fine. Communication is the transmission, receipt and processing of information in the form of hard data, ideas, feelings and impressions. Through this process, people receive information from their environment.   They process this information, make decisions about their future actions and send information back.   Communication shapes the way we relate to the world.   It is an ongoing, dynamic process that happens whether we are aware of it or not.

What people call poor communication isn't a failure of people to transmit, receive or process information.   When people are complaining about poor communication what they are usually objecting to is the nature of the information they receive.

One company with which I worked was noted by its staff for its 'poor communication'. The managing director, they complained, behaved as though he didn't like people. If he was getting into the lift and someone else joined him he would get out and take the stairs. He avoided eye contact, discussion and kept all information to himself. Only the few people with whom he felt safe were told vital strategic information and they, following his lead, didn't pass the information on. The people who weren't in the managing director's inner circle protested that in a climate of such poor communication it was impossible for them to know what was happening and make rational decisions.

It seemed to me that what the managing director was communicating very clearly was that in his organisation people weren't liked or trusted. Through his way of operating, the managing director set a clear role model that relationships didn't matter, information was to be hidden and those in power had no need to grow or learn. It will come as little surprise to you that the company in question had poor customer service, high staff turnover and appalling information systems. The place was crawling with consultants, all of whom were briefed to fix the problems and none of whom were given the information, support or time to allow them to do so. The company buzzed with activity and everybody knew what game they had to play to survive. Interestingly, this organisation was an average performer in its service-based industry.

They're just following our lead

Due to our own lack of self-awareness, most of us leaders don't realise that the things we criticise in the people we lead are mere reflections of our own personal traits and behaviours. We all communicate all the time. The trouble is that most of us don't know what we are communicating. However, the people who depend on us for direction watch us very closely. It's in their best interests to know our foibles, interests, preferences and habits. It's as though to them the leader's behaviour and style is magnified many times, as if looked at through a telescope. For the leader, looking back through the telescope from the small end, everything about their followers is diminished. Looking through the telescope from their perspective it is hard for a leader to realise how powerfully they and their actions are magnified. Leaders thus undervalue the effect of their ability to role model behaviour attitudes and changes.

Role modelling is no less effective when the changes in question are to do with personal characteristics and ways of thinking. A game I enjoy playing with groups of executives involves sitting people in small clusters and asking them to visualise each other as animals. I then have them report their fantasies to the group along with why they chose those animals. What amazes people is the incredible accuracy with which people can describe personal traits about each other, *even when they haven't previously met*. We communicate so much about ourselves in so many different ways, and when we are a leader let me assure you that people notice and take heed, down to the smallest detail. There is no stronger change mechanism than the leader being different.

The jargon calls it 'living the message' or 'walking your talk'. We all live our message all the time and often our message is that we don't live up to our own words. When this happens, the message we send is that we are hypocrites, untruthful and not to be trusted. We fail to realise that people are more likely to follow our lead rather than obey our commands.

If your people aren't behaving the way that you want them to, look to your own behaviour—you'll be surprised what you will find.

Becoming a safe person

As we have already seen, most organisations are not safe places for people to risk being different. Most leaders do not have the understanding, personal insight and self-acceptance to allow others to explore the path to real change in safety. Intuitively, everybody knows this and is therefore provided with a perfect excuse to stay the same. The leader then complains about the difficulty in getting people to change.

The fact is that by not opening to growth, learning and personal development, people in most organisations are making what appears to be a very rational decision. For people to change they need some level of safety. The further along the growth path you move, the more this safety comes from your own competence and inner strength. In the early days you need safe people to help you create your safety. The most powerful safe person to have is the leader, for it is he or she who creates the environment in which people are to operate. If we want ongoing change to be part of that operation, we need to ensure that the environment we create is a safe one.

A safe-environment is one in which

- you are accepted for yourself
- your emotions are validated
- people listen to you
- other people are real with you
- there are clear and appropriate boundaries
- communication is direct and open
- your humanity is supported
- people are honest
- agendas are open, not hidden

- expectations are clearly expressed
- confidences are respected
- people mean what they say

Safe environments are created by safe people. Being a safe person doesn't mean being an emotional namby-pamby. On the contrary, because they are very real, safe people are particularly strong. Martin Luther King is on record as saying that leadership is about being 'strong-minded and tenderhearted'—that's a pretty good description of a safe person.

Setting limits

One of the characteristics of safe people is an ability to be true to themselves. This means knowing who they are, what they want and setting their limits. Over the years I have found that nothing creates a feeling of safety in a corporate group more strongly than a chief executive clearly and honesty expressing his or her limits.

One of my clients is noted for his meanness. I remember seeing a look of great admiration and relief on the faces of his corporate group when he admitted that he had 'short arms and long pockets' and stated that he saw his acute sense of economy as an integral part of his leadership style. He went on to note that one of his key priorities was that people kept control on spending, right down to the paper clips. It wasn't that people liked his fixation with costs but they felt safe knowing that this was a limit outside which it was dangerous for them to tread.

Some years ago I was working with the top team of a government bureaucracy helping them devise a corporate strategy. There was one member of that team who kept asking difficult questions, raising constant objections and generally blocking the proceedings. When I asked him why he was doing these things he claimed that he was 'trying to be helpful'. I noted that I wasn't finding him the least bit helpful and would rather that he changed his behaviour. At this he denounced the whole process claiming it a farce. He insisted the chief executive had already decided what strategy he wanted and had simply employed me to con everybody else into agreeing.

There was, in fact, a large amount of truth in this remark. The chief executive had prepared his own strategic plan and handed it to me prior to the workshop. He was very clear about wanting a number of major changes in the organisation. Where he was unclear was in how these changes might take place. He and I had talked this out. I had no wish to be used to manipulate people into believing they had a say in something that had been decided.

In answer to his subordinate's objections, the chief executive explained that some matters were open for negotiation and some weren't. He then stated explicitly where his limits lay. The chief executive asked his managers for their input and assistance in the areas on which he was unclear and they were pleased to give it. Again it wasn't that people necessarily liked what the chief executive had decided—in some cases they obviously didn't—but they valued being given the respect and decency of being told the truth and knowing within which boundaries they could safely operate.

Giving feedback

Safe people are not afraid to give honest feedback. This is in itself rare. What makes safe people even rarer is their ability to give the feedback in a way that leaves the receiver with full information, dignity and choice.

Some years ago I worked with the senior executives of two major government departments helping them put in an Executive Performance Feedback System. As part of this assignment I had to interview a large number of senior bureaucrats. My strongest memory from these interviews was the high number of people who claimed to never having being told how their work and behaviour was affecting those around them, including their employer. Rather than being frightened of feedback, these executives were hungry for it. They wanted to know where they stood with regard to the important people in their work environment.

Time and time again I have worked with groups of executives who will happily pull a colleague, boss or subordinate to pieces in their absence and refuse to provide the object of their derision any concrete feedback face to face, even when requested to do so.

Constructive feedback provides people with an impetus to change. By providing people with a concrete example of their behaviour, followed up by a clear indication of how that behaviour has effected us and what we would like, we give people the opportunity to decide for themselves whether the effect they are having is the effect they desire. This is information that few of us ever receive and most of us value if it is given in a way that helps us to see that we, as a person, are valued, even if there is something about our current behaviour and beliefs that is causing some problems.

There are many books on management and communication that lay out techniques for giving feedback and I don't intend to reproduce them here. In terms of skills I think you can't go much past 'I' Statements provided in page 88, chapter 3, and the listening skills referred to later in this chapter. However, skills alone don't make feedback easier.

Every time we give someone feedback we are telling them

something about ourselves. We are saying:

- These are things to which I pay attention.
- These are the things I like and don't like.
- These are the things that affect me.
- This is how these things affect me.
- This is what I would like done about it.

All this involves a level of courage, honesty and concern for relationships that is rare in public life. It also necessitates a degree of environmental awareness and self-perception that many leaders simply don't possess.   Thankfully we can all learn to be more aware, more honest and more caring. I'm not saying that it is easy but it is possible and it's worth the effort if what you want is to help people grow and change.

Being compassionate

In her book *The Dance of Intimacy*, Dr Harriet Goldhor Lerner writes of the phenomenon of change and change back. The way I picture this is as follows. Person A and person B are waltzing together. Suddenly, for some reason of their own, person A starts to rumba. This presents person B with a dilemma—do they continue waltzing or do they, too, adopt a different step.

Of course there are a huge number of variables involved in what happens next. Is the music different? Can they both hear the music? Is there some other reason to rumba? Do they both know how to rumba? How well do they know each other? Is this an ongoing relationship? Do they intend to dance together again? In the meantime, there is likely to be considerable resistance on the part of person B to stop waltzing.

When most of us decide to change, for reasons that seem perfectly good to us, we get annoyed when the people to whom we relate resist our changes.   A well-reported hindrance to the recovery of those with a drug or alcohol addiction is the people who love them.   Although for years these people may have complained about the behaviour of the addict, when that behaviour changes it alters the nature of the relationship, thus putting pressure on their loved ones to adapt and themselves to be different.   It is not uncommon for the spouses of recovering alcoholics to encourage their partners to have another drink.

This pattern is true for all relationships.   When we start to change, the people around us will instinctively attempt to get us to go back to the way we were before so that they don't have to change in the way they relate to us.   This is the dance of change back.

To deal with this situation, we need to develop compassion.

When we start speaking our truth, setting our limits and giving constructive feedback, we can expect people to kick up.   We are not behaving 'normally', we are different.   Our difference is likely to arouse the unconscious fears of those around us.   Fearful people, as we have seen, often behave in rather unpleasant and unconstructive ways.   Our habitual response to this kind of behaviour is to go into our DEFENDED YOU and hit, hurt and push back, all of which aggravates the situation.

When, however, you are well down the track in your own learning, when you yourself have experienced your own change from a stance of emotional openness and awareness, you understand to your core how hard and painful change can be.   You know how it is to be fearful, uncertain and challenged outside of your comfort zone.

From this stance you can relate to the other as a human being.   You can understand and relate to the source of their behaviour.   You can resist the temptation to defend and thus remain available to provide the other with the emotional support and understanding they need to travel the rocky path of change.

Where setting your limits and providing constructive feedback provide the impetuses that propel people towards change, compassion provides the understanding and support that makes change possible and desirable. What you are saying is, 'I understand and care for you', 'I know what it is like to change'. 'I support your attempts to grow and change'. This provides a pull towards embracing difference.

Listening

Safe people are great listeners. People who know how to listen, really listen, are incredibly rare. We are all so bound up in our own thoughts and our own neuroses that we rarely actually hear what another person is saying. Sometimes we aren't even aware that another person is talking.

Yet listening to another person is one of the greatest ways of developing open and cooperative relationships. Really listening provides you with increased information about yourself, other people and the world. Nobody is better informed than the person who truly listens. Moreover, being listened to, really heard, is such a rare and wonderful experience that people will seek out a listener again and again. They will express to the listener their inner thoughts and feelings, forging a bond between listener and talker. If you want people to choose to follow you down a different path, to want to grow, change and cooperate—listen to them.

Now, real listening is very difficult for most of us. Real listening involves letting go of our preconceptions of who the other is, what they are saying and why they are saying it. It means coming out from behind our DEFENDED YOU and listening from our essence, thus letting in what the speaker has to say.

Real listening involves not trying to impress, help, correct, fix up, advise, reassure or protect. It involves allowing ourselves to be present, real and human, without preconceptions and judgements.

When we really listen, we simply put ourselves in the other person's shoes and begin to understand how it is for them, what it is that they are feeling, wanting, thinking and experiencing. You help the other person explore their own humanity by going on the journey with them.

I remember working with a group of executives and having them practise a listening exercise. Because some of them found this too confronting, I asked for volunteers. Two fellows happily obliged and resumed a conversation they had started the day before about their different ways of handling a union dispute that had arisen. The conversation moved between the executives with them both stating their arguments and trying to convince the other to change his mind. It was obvious that neither one was listening. I then asked the executives to change their intention to one of learning. Their only function was to really hear what the other person had to say and to discover how it was for the other and why they felt so strongly about the issue.

Very quickly the mood of the whole room changed. The points of the argument seemed to fall away as the executives began to connect as human beings. Within a short time, the audience began to feel uncomfortable because of the intimacy that was arising from our 'actors'. A feeling that we could only describe as love began to fill the room. Some months later, when the union dispute rose again, these two men provided each other with what one called 'the most support I have ever received'. Simply by listening to each other, the differences were resolved and a lasting relationship was built.

The experience of listening can be life-changing. The more easily we can drop our DEFENDED YOU and be human with another person, the more powerful will be the effects of our listening.

When people are listened to they solve their own problems, work through their own issues, face their own truths and become more real themselves. They open to change and growth and become committed to you and your leadership. They grow to trust you, respect you and seek your guidance.

We all find it easier to listen when we feel safe. When someone is attacking us it is more difficult to stay open and just listen. Yet at no time is doing just that more useful, important and effective.

It is not at all uncommon when I am doing my pre–workshop interviews, when they meet me for the first time, for executives to launch into heated attacks on me, the work I do and consultants in general. I have often been told by executives that they consider talking to me a waste of time and paying me a waste of money. I am berated, lectured, undermined and ridiculed. On such occasions I remind myself that the behaviour I am witnessing results from fear, and that beneath this boisterous defence are some aching emotional wounds and a wonderful human being. I also remind myself that if I listen, really listen, I will gain both information and access to the human being. So I ask questions like, 'Why do you think that this is a waste of time and money?' I search for the cause of the upset. I am genuinely interested and open to learning. And learn I do, about myself, about the other person and about the issues that will help me in the assignment ahead. What is interesting is that it is these individuals who often become my biggest supporters and promoters. Because I have seen past their DEFENDED YOU , listened to what they had to say and not rejected them for sharing their truth, I have earned their loyalty. Listening allows us to do that.

True listening is based on the premise that your reality is true for you and that it is a privilege for another person to share your reality with you. It is impossible to really listen to another person's truth without being changed by it. Sharing another person's reality for even a few moments broadens our own perspective of how life and others are. Every time we really listen we become more than we were before. It's almost as if by making room for the truth of another we stretch our limits so that there is more room for us, for life and humanity.

One of the biggest blocks to really listening to another person is to think that for us to be of value we have to do something, say something or in some way contribute. If, however we fill the space with our contribution, we rob the other person of room to explore for themselves. In this way we rob ourselves of the privilege of seeing into another person's world and learning from it.

Listening doesn't involve giving up yourself, your agenda or your goals. It simply acknowledges that you are more likely to gain other people's support if you can encompass their world. By listening, you increase your knowledge and understanding of your environment and the strengths and weaknesses of your relationships within that environment. You create safety and pave the way for change. There is plenty of time to express your agenda after you have listened to others.

Creating space for change to happen

Real change involves people taking a step back and looking at what they want and how their current patterns of thinking, feeling and acting will aid or impair their quest to reach their goal. Because most of us are so unskilled at noticing our patterns and dealing with our emotions, this can be a time-consuming and slow process.

Most leaders are particularly busy. Moreover, they create 'busi-ness' around them, which often precludes the possibility for them and others to do any real growing and learning. Without time and space for reflection, experiment and processing new material, you can be sure that any change will be cosmetic—a mere rearrangement of the same constituent parts.

If we are to move past the energy–consuming and limited bounds of the DEFENDED YOU into the richness of clarity, creativity and energy that lie in our ESSENTIAL YOU, we have to create time and space for change. As leaders, by creating such time we not only create ourselves as powerful role models but we also push responsibility down the line to where it belongs, thus affording our people an opportunity to grow. Moreover, if we are to become safe people we need time and space to nurture ourselves back to fullness, to heal our own WOUNDED YOU and to ensure that we have the emotional strength and energy that we will need to lead through times of change.

Delegation

The first step in delegating is making the decision that we are willing to take responsibility for ourselves. We begin to acknowledge that we and our time are too valuable to waste. Leadership is about being a role model, creating an environment in which people can flourish and setting strategic direction. Our sanest investment of time is in creating ourselves as effective leaders.

Once people decide to delegate they are usually faced with a whole bevy of obstacles, all of which seem insurmountable. Firstly, it appears that no one is available, willing or capable of doing our work. Secondly, we don't have the time to train people or the ability to tolerate their mistakes while they learn, and even if we did no one would do things as well as us.

I once had a summer job working for an eminent professor.

This professor was one of the smartest guys I've ever met. His ability to think through difficult problems, analyse vast sums of ambiguous and conflicting data and make rational decisions was first-rate. His colleagues and staff so valued his advice and ability that they delegated to him huge numbers of decisions and projects. Knowing that he was indeed smarter than those around him, this professor took on task after task.

Walking into the professor's office, it was almost impossible to find him; he was constantly buried behind a huge pile of files and he was always weeks, sometimes months, behind with his work, although he worked 60 to 70 hours a week. He might have been the best and the brightest but he was also the most exhausted, the most behind in his own projects and the most abused for his tardiness.

Until we have the courage and perseverance to notice our own patterns of thought and behaviour, we won't know how much of our indispensability is real. Most of the reasons people give for not delegating seem awfully real to them but are really delusions of self-grandeur, political ploys or excuses for not facing up to their own issues and problems. While ever we are unaware we can fool ourselves. While ever we continue to fool ourselves we can remain unaware.

The next step, then, is to continue to raise our awareness. As we do this we will find that we are nowhere near as indispensable as we thought. We also need to be clear as to our priorities. What are the things that we want to do, that we think are important and essential for us, the leader, to do? Part of this is realising that the more responsibilities we take, the fewer we leave for others. Our 'excellence' may be stunting the growth of those below us.

Having come to terms with this, we can start pushing work out to others who may happily accept it or may fall into the change-back response.

There is no earthly reason why people who have become used to having us do everything for them are going to welcome our decision not to do that any more. When we change, for our good reasons, those with whom we relate will have change forced on them. Even people who have been asking for change are likely to baulk once we grant them their requested opportunities. Once we start to delegate, people around us have to learn to set their priorities, learn new skills, organise their time and become more responsible. If our staff, family and friends are 'normal', you can expect them to act helpless, aggressive, resistant and unhelpful, in fact to do everything in their power to get us to go back to being the way we were. Many of us find this reassuring because it provides us with the encouragement we need to revert to old habits.

If we are clear about what we want, sure about our rights to enjoy life and peace of mind, we will be able to stay resolute yet open-hearted. This will allow others to adjust to our changes at their own pace.

The next obstacle to delegation is the compulsion to 'save' people. When we start to delegate, those around us will be stretched and challenged. So many managers at this stage query their right to be a leader as against a doer of tasks. They begin to feel guilty that they are moving towards the more nebulous strategic areas while their staff are taking on more tangible duties. To alleviate their own doubts and to remove the discomfort of their people, the manager decides delegation doesn't work and restores the status quo. There is a common myth that busy people achieve, when in fact 'busi–ness' is often an excuse for lack of strategic vision, clear thought and fully functioning relationships.

However, the more persistent and committed keep on. They spend time listening to people's concerns and worries, then clearly state their own needs and limits. They support people by training them into new skills, thus themselves growing in personal awareness, relationship and communication. When we help others to deal with their change, our growth will be promoted and we will end up with more of *us*, better relationships, more time and a more effective operation.

The final challenge to delegation is possibly the biggest. This is learning to cope with having less to do. When leaders are successful in delegating, they often feel guilty that they aren't busy all the time. They start to question their own worthiness. So many of us correlate our own worth with our level of 'busi-ness' that when we get to be less busy we think we are less worthy.

In fact the opposite is true—as we become less busy we have the opportunity to become more strategic. We can be wiser, smarter and more effective in both choosing what we do and in doing it. This is another step in our becoming more self-determining and, like all steps in the growth process, we can expect to suffer from our own change-back response. We will begin to notice every mistake made by the people to whom we delegate while downplaying their successes. We will question our own sanity and wait for the disasters to happen. A good antidote for this is to ask:

- How do I feel?
- Will this enhance my peace?
- What do I want?

These simple questions will help you to notice your own patterns and to make decisions about your actions, based on real information rather than fuzzy 'old brain' responses. You have moved one step further to Peaceful Chaos and strategic being.

Everybody is different

One of the things that made delegation easier for me was the realisation that people are different. Not only are we all good at different things, we actually enjoy doing different kinds of work and operating in different ways.

Based on the work of Jung , the mother and daughter team of Myers and Briggs found that people have different preferences for the way they deal with reality. They organised these preferences along four different continuums which give us a good insight into how we all differ.

Internals versus externals

Some of us prefer to be introverted in our relationships. We like to work things out in our own minds before we discuss them with others. We are the quiet achievers, the thinkers and planners of this world. External preference people, however, prefer to work through their ideas while talking. These are the people who prefer to deliver addresses impromptu, who are gregarious and happy to be constantly interrupted. Externals love internals because they listen while the externals talk through their ideas. In fact externals often have difficulty having ideas unless they can talk them through. Internals have no difficulty thinking through their ideas, their problem is talking about them, particularly without preparation.

Knowing about internals and externals I understood why some people so easily took the floor while others sat back. It wasn't that the talkers had the best ideas, it was that they liked to talk and the listeners preferred to listen than to have to talk themselves. It also explained why so many people send out bits of paper that I, an external, never read. We all like to communicate differently and that difference is a blessing because it provides us with complementary skills and interests.

Intuitives versus sensates

The next continuum is based on how we process information. Those who are intuitive look for and see the big picture. They never let a fact or detail get in the way of a good idea or vision. Intuitives are the world's dreamers, creators and visionaries. They hate routine work and are always looking for a new way, a new idea or a creative solution. They drive sensates mad. Someone with a sensate preference likes details, sticking to a plan and working with tangibles. The schedules that intuitives ignore were probably prepared by sensates. Intuitives often see sensates as boring, limited and preoccupied with detail and trivia. Sensates find intuitives unpredictable, unreliable and with their head in the clouds. Intuitives and sensates are two halves of the one puzzle. The big picture doesn't work without the details, and the details take you nowhere without the big picture. As a highly intuitive individual, I found it a great blessing that there were people around who actually enjoy detailed work and do it well. I immediately went out and found some sensates to help me do the areas of my work that I hated and did very badly. This freed me from hundreds of hours of tedium while producing far superior results than I could ever have achieved alone. With the extra available time, I was able to develop my skills, talents and sense of self. The result was that I made more profits.

Thinkers versus feelers

Discovering the differences between thinkers and feelers was another great boon to my being able to delegate more. Thinkers process their information through their brain first and then through their emotions. Feelers process through their emotions and then through their brains. As both thinkers and feelers in our society have restricted access to their emotions and ESSENTIAL YOU, neither does a better job of processing information than the other. They do, however, make decisions quite differently. Feelers operate very much in terms of their subjective response. They know what they want, what they like and what they believe is right. They have strong principles and will fight for them. They are usually perceived as warm, if somewhat enigmatic, individuals who bring their own charisma and flavour to everything they do. Thinkers, on the other hand, are very rational and objective about everything. They are great on cost benefit analysis and are very pragmatic about their decision–making, based on the logic of the situation.

To the feeler, the thinker appears cold, hard and unprincipled. To the thinker, the feeler appears overly committed to the rights and wrongs of any issue and insufficiently businesslike in their approach. Again, both are each other's blessing. For me, to know that I could delegate research and analysis to people who preferred it, was wonderful. To the thinker, being able to use the warmth and charisma of the feeler can save years of trying to be something you just aren't. I now quite happily leave accounting to the accountant, business management to the business manager and research to my assistant. I do what I'm good at. We all tend to be good at the things that we most enjoy. Who was it who said that the lucky person is one who can make their vocation their vacation?

Judgers versus perceivers

This final continuum is also a boon when it comes to delegating. Those of us with a perceptive preference enjoy going with the flow of life. When we go on holidays, we prefer not to plan our journey but take it as it comes. We love ambiguity, change and paradox. We are the world's change agents. We are also disorganised, unmethodical and prone to information overload. This means that we are often seen as indecisive.

Those with a judging preference, however, love plans, clear and measurable deadlines and often make decisions way before all the information is to hand. They have clear—if sometimes misguided—ideas about what is right and wrong and act quickly on their decisions. This means that the people with the best ideas aren't necessarily the people most prone to action. Again, this presents a very good opportunity for shared effort and delegation.

Teamwork

Looked at from this perspective, delegation is not something to be limited to those we supervise. Teams can benefit greatly by knowing the strengths, weaknesses and preferences of their members and allocating tasks to the people who are most suitable and most interested. In teams where everybody has similar preferences, delegation to outsiders such as support staff and consultants becomes even more crucial. Not only does this give us more time to concentrate on what we like, it also ensures that we end up with a superior result.

Catalysing change

Peaceful Chaos leadership is notably different from management as most of us have experienced it. Unlike traditional management, Peaceful Chaos leadership is based on the reality that events and people cannot be controlled either now or in the future. Rather than wasting huge amounts of time and energy trying to get the world to go our way, Peaceful Chaos leadership accepts that people and the world will be themselves. Leadership is about working out what you want, showing that it is possible and setting an example that people will want to follow. Leadership in times of change also involves creating around you an environment in which people feel motivated, safe and sufficiently supported to want to grow, learn and give of their best. This same environment supports people to take responsibility for their own thoughts, feelings and actions, and therefore means change can and will take place quickly when and where it is needed.

I am a professional change agent. People pay me to help them change. It took me some time to realise that the most effective way I could help anyone change was to accept people exactly as they were. By doing this I created an environment safe enough for people to want to change themselves.

Clients have described my role as that of a catalyst. As I wrote earlier, a catalyst promotes a process but is not consumed by that process. A catalyst does this by being itself. Just by the nature of what it is, a catalyst encourages change to happen around it. My job and that of any leader in times of rapid change is to make change easier, that is to be a catalyst. This means growing and changing in such a way that our very presence sparks and sustains a process of growth and change in the people around us.

In old-style management our focus was on other people. Our efforts went into trying to get people to think and act in ways that we, the manager, thought were appropriate. In Peaceful Chaos leadership our focus is on ourselves, ensuring that we have the necessary inner resources, insight, love, honesty and openness to learning. This will allow us to model learning and growth, as well as create and sustain fulfilling and productive relationships. As a catalyst our two most important functions are to promote a process and to look after ourselves. A catalyst that is consumed by the process ceases to be of use. It is essential therefore that we be ourself, 100 per cent, and take responsibility for our own well-being.

I spend at least 10 hours a week ensuring that I am not consumed by the process of change. I meditate at least once a day. Every day I take a long bath, I walk 20 to 30 minutes a day and have a spiritual practice that takes about half-an-hour daily. I go to supervision twice a week to receive personal support and professional backup for the work I do, and I belong to two support groups. I regularly work through personal development and spiritual growth exercises that I find in personal development and inspirational books.

I do not spend all this time on myself because I am in need of help, or because I am a particularly selfish person. I do it because I value my own well-being and find that nurturing myself enhances my peace of mind. By operating from a state of peace I am able to offer my family, my clients, my friends and my staff the kind of leadership I believe that they deserve. By nurturing my own well-being I also ensure that I am not consumed by the many change processes that I catalyse. By being responsible for me I encourage the people around me to take the same level of responsibility for themselves, to support their own growth and learning. The more they do this, the more discretionary time we all create.

Changing whole organisations

All the above processes work. They don't, however, work quickly. Many of my clients find when it comes to passing the benefits they are receiving on to their people, that their impatience outstrips the speed of their own growth. We have, therefore, come up with some compromises.

At the same time as I work with the leaders I also work with a group of in–house change agents, helping them develop introductory programs that they can take to the whole organisation. We also begin a process to assist these in–house change agents to work towards developing their own abilities as role models, safe people and catalysts of change.

I also encourage each organisation to develop its own change program. By developing the change program in–house we ensure that it is matched to the growing awareness and skills of the organisation's members and its appropriate current and envisaged needs. A program designed by an organisation's executives is more likely to have the support and ownership that will be needed to last during the long haul of change. This ensures that the organisation grows alongside its leaders in a way that is compatible with the leaders, their growth and vision.

An effective change program takes years, and things don't stand still in the interim. Most of my clients are highly successful business and government leaders and know well how to play the accepted management games. It is usual during the time that I work with any organisation that they undergo restructures, downsizing, market repositioning and all the commonly accepted changes that organisations face. What is different is that as time passes these changes become easier to formulate and to implement. Change becomes an accepted part of life. Resistance to change begins to fall away and it is seen as an opportunity rather than a threat. Moreover, as leaders become more self–determining they are in a better position to ensure that all changes they instigate are necessary, appropriate to their needs and tailored to suit them, their leadership style and their strategic objectives.

There is no less chaos or change in those who have embraced Peaceful Chaos. It is just that, for them, it's all part of life and they have grown to allow reality with all its ups and downs to contribute to their peace and well–being.

Conclusion

If any one had told me in advance how difficult it would be to write a book such as this, I would never have believed them. It wasn't so much the discipline of spending weeks at the computer or the intellectual challenge of getting my mind around the material. It wasn't even the seemingly impossible task of putting a highly nebulous, experiential approach to change onto paper. The biggest challenge for me was the impact that writing this book had on my own self-awareness and growth.

For me, like my clients, growth and change is a process. Learning lies in observing that process. As I wrote, I triggered my own defences and my own WOUNDED YOU. I found myself unearthing 'old brain' fears and hurts as well as the joy and delight of new insight. This is the same process that happens when I work with my clients. I am sure that the person who learns the most through my work is me.

Real change is very much a matter of relationships. I find it impossible to work with people who are changing without being changed myself. There is a dynamic that happens around change that touches everybody. When I am working with a client, I feel this particularly because I am working with the client, their issues, their problems and their ideas. The material to hand is their material not mine. My ideas and inputs are offered in response to the client's expressed needs and objectives.

In writing this book I wasn't able to elicit from you, the reader, your situation, needs and desires. I was able to share with you my experiences and those of others, but I was not able to offer you direct feedback.

I hope that the exercises I have included will help you begin your own process, raise you own awareness and send you on the search for your own answers. I hope you look for and find a safe person help you on your journey.

I realise that I haven't prescribed the answers, because I sincerely believe that the only answer that will work for you is one that you will work out for yourself. All I or anyone else can do is to act as a catalyst, a support, a bringer of new ideas and a provider of feedback. I hope you can now go out and find many of these things for yourself.

Living in the essence

Writing this book has helped me to put into perspective so many of the things that I have experienced in my own life and with my clients over the past 7 years. It has helped me to see how incredibly difficult and yet how vital it is to mix our personal well-being and inner strength with our day-to-day business life and success. I am more and more convinced that those who live in their DEFENDED YOU may get to the top but will find it increasingly difficult to stay there. It won't just be business imperatives that will undermine those who don't mellow and grow, they will be vulnerable on all sides. Their health, marriage and emotional stability will be at risk unless they find some way of maintaining their peace in what can only be times of increasing pressure and change ahead.

We can no longer expect stability in any area of our lives. We can anticipate changing our employers, careers, homes and relationships almost as a matter of course. Nobody's life will be untouched by death, illness and tragedy. We can expect that we or someone we love will be the victim of abuse, alcoholism, drug dependence or nervous breakdown.

We all have a choice. We can embrace life for what it is and capitalise on it, or we can deny reality and fight to have the world be different. This choice is expressed in the serenity prayer.

> God grant me the serenity
> to accept the things I cannot change,
> the courage to change the things I can
> and the wisdom to know the difference.

Peaceful Chaos is the art of having the acceptance, courage and wisdom to know where to most usefully apply our energy so that we can capitalise on life as it is. Chaos is given, peace comes from developing the personal awareness and characteristics to have us flow with the tide of life, not stand our ground and fight against the inevitable. This is a very personal choice with huge public implications. If we as a society continue to operate from our DEFENDED YOU rather than develop and grow from the wholeness of our being, we will never find solutions to the major problems that face us. As the complexity of our society increases, we need to find ways of maintaining our perspective, our balance and our values.

We must all do this as individuals and then have the courage to share our decisions and truths with others. We can go on battling, destroying each other in wars and through political wrangling, or we can take the risk of finding another way, a human way, a way that brings us peace, joy and life, a way based on growth, learning and change. Like the search for the Holy Grail, there is no reason to believe that the way will be easy, comfortable or safe. But who said anything worth having comes cheaply?

From my own experience I can say that the more you move into the fullness of life, living and your own ESSENTIAL YOU, the more you want. From time to time I step back and look at the wonder that is my life and ask how I, already having so much, can want more. Then I remind myself that life is an ongoing process of growth. Growth is about being more of who I am in every aspect of my being. So I relax and enjoy what I have while making room for more.

I hope this book will send you on a search for your own answers. I also hope that I have been able to convince you that all that really matters is the search—what you discover is the icing on the cake. The pleasure and the learning lie in the process not the content. Life lies in the unfolding, in the discovering, in the searching, in the relating, in the noticing, in the communicating—life lies in the living.

We accord so much legitimacy to stored information in the form of books, videos and cassettes and yet stored information is of little use to us. Its only benefit lies in how we process that information—in the dynamics of our thought processes, in our emotional responses and in how we incorporate that information into our lives. Yet these are the things we miss or see as irrelevant. Time and again when I have encouraged groups of executives to reflect on the process that we are experiencing, I am stunned not only by how incredibly bad they are at it but also how noisily and aggressively they resist the opportunity to reflect on their lives. Having worked now with so many very successful people I am sure that this resistance is due to the fact that to stop and notice would be to acknowledge the emptiness and paucity of their lives. It is only by not noticing what they are doing, how they are doing it and how it feels to be them that they can continue to carry on the charade they call life. If they were to notice the reality they would feel impelled to change.

Yet the path to Peaceful Chaos can only be trodden by living in the process. The path is like that of an atom: it is constantly moving, constantly changing and impossible to measure. Yet it is very real, it is just outside of our normal vision and comprehension. So we need to learn new ways of seeing and spend time not knowing while we learn to broaden our perspective. Meanwhile, we need to get our old perspective out of the way sufficiently to ensure it doesn't interfere with our ability to encompass new realities.

The path of an atom is something we can think about rationally, the path of our own life is a much more subjective matter. When we are expanding to deal with new ways of being we have to deal with a whole range of emotional baggage as well as expanding our intellectual horizons. The intellectual part usually seems easy compared to the difficulty of working with our damaged, uncontrollable and totally nebulous emotions.

It is in dealing with the emotional healing and growth that ensures that you need good company on the path of Peaceful Chaos. You need safe people to walk beside you. These may be therapists, safe consultants or people like yourself who are a little further down the track. You need friends for support but you also need older hands for insight and guidance. It is important, however, that you retain responsibility for the process and what you obtain from it. This is your life, your growth and your well–being—never give that responsibility away to any one.

In walking my path to Peaceful Chaos I also found that I needed more than human assistance. If I was going to give up my need to control, if I was going to trust the process and if I was going to risk letting down my defences, I needed to believe that I was going to be looked after. I needed to trust in a power greater than myself. Of course, I wasn't the first to find this. All the programs, such as the Twelve Step Program of Alcoholics Anonymous, are based on the principle that to overcome self–defeating patterns and make our lives work we need to place our trust in a Higher Power. Although I rarely recommend that my clients pursue a spiritual path, I have noticed that some time down the road to growth they make this discovery for themselves.

Relating to a Higher Power lightens our load when the going gets tough, and makes the impossible achievable. My spiritual life has greatly enhanced my being. It has helped me to gain sustenance and support when all else seemed to have failed. When I feel very judgemental, I look at a group of flowers and wonder if you can judge nature's creations. When I feel pain, I tell myself that I don't have to suffer alone, help is always available.

When I am working with my clients and I have absolutely no idea what to do next I look to my Higher Power for guidance. I can then let go and let whatever happens happen. When I am tired or feeling low I walk outside and notice the birds, the trees, the flowers and the sky and remember that there is so much to enjoy, so much wonder, life and abundance. I see the energy and love on my children's faces and marvel at the miracle of life.

When I work with new clients I notice how little value they seem to place on life, themselves and each other—it's as though nothing is sacred. To me everything is sacred, every place is a sacred place and every person is a child of God. There is a Navajo Prayer that goes like this:

Happily may I walk.
May it be beautiful before me,
May it be beautiful behind me,
May it be beautiful below me,
May it be beautiful above me,
May it be beautiful all around me,
In beauty it is finished.

Walking through life in connection with a power greater than ourselves helps us to notice the beauty at every turn. Our belief encourages us to stop and notice the wonder of the world in which we live, the beauty of life and of living.

One of my clients once remarked, 'You know, Margot, you shouldn't exist.   You're a woman in business, encouraging us to discover all of ourselves. You help us to see our humanity and to embrace our essence in a context where all of that is completely alien.' This same client some time later told me that he had felt a huge weight come off his shoulders as he had learnt to reconcile the parts of himself that had previously been in conflict. He had denied himself the right to experience his humanity and his 'God self' at work. This denial had cost him dearly in terms of stress, limited thought and stunted relationships. By allowing for the possibility of there being more, he had become more.

I find many people have been turned away from religion because of unhappy and even damaging experiences they have had earlier in life.   To throw away a spiritual belief because of what some people have done in the name of religion seems to be counterproductive. I find that my belief provides me with constant companionships, constant guidance and a constant reminder that I am loved, lovable and worthy of a full and rich life. It also reminds me that I am only one of nature's creations.

When I am tempted to mistreat myself through overwork,

overstress or overindulgence, I remind myself that as one of nature's children I am worthy of love and respect. It is my responsibility to look after myself.

The path to Peaceful Chaos is the path to living at peace with the world. It is not a path of escape or defence but a way to access and employ the potential that lies within each person, each organisation and each community. It is a different path, an uncertain path, a risky path and yet once you start to walk it and feel its benefits, you will wonder why it took you so long to begin.

Glossary

BEING PRESENT   the ability to stay in the ESSENTIAL YOU moment by moment

CATALYST   an agent that promotes a process but is not consumed by that process

CHANGE AGENT   a person who encourages and supports desired changes in the way individuals think, feel and act in an organisational setting

CONTROL   to dominate and command others. This gives the illusion of strategy and leadership but really takes away people's self–responsibility and fosters dependency

DEFENDED YOU   the mask which defends and protects us, often unconsciously

DEPENDENT   emotionally reliant on the approval and consent of others

DYSFUNCTIONAL FAMILY   a family that does not provide a safe environment for the 'psychological and spiritual well–being and growth of each of its members'

ESSENTIAL YOU   our real self, genetic inheritance and the source of our creative and potential energy

FOLLOW OUR OWN LEAD   the act of contacting and trusting the messages from the ESSENTIAL YOU and using them as the basis for personal decision–making and action

GOOD BOY/GIRL   behaving in a manner to please others, irrespective of the efficacy or personal fulfilment gained from such behaviour

ILLUSIONS   games played by DEFENDED YOU and WOUNDED YOU to stop us seeing and accepting reality

INNER KNOWING an acceptance of reality that comes from ESSENTIAL YOU, by-passing the repression, denial and other games of WOUNDED and DEFENDED YOU. It's when we trust our inner knowing that we start to follow our own lead

INTUITION insights and inspiration from ESSENTIAL YOU. When accepted our intuition becomes our inner knowing and forms the basis of following our own lead

MANIPULATION the process of tricking, beguiling, seducing, forcing or intimidating others into fulfilling our dreams, expectations or desires

MISSION an organisation's reason for being. It is most effectively stated in a way that stimulates pride and motivation in each and every organisational member

NOT KNOWING an honest and very common state of being, all too rarely admitted which makes room for new ideas, feelings and actions

OLD BRAIN repository of childhood thoughts, feelings and images, which nonetheless have a timeless aspect and can dramatically affect how we behave as adults

ORGANISATIONAL
CHANGE the process of how an organisation adapts to the growing and conflicting demands of a world which is changing increasingly fast

PEACEFUL
CHAOS the art of leadership in times of rapid change

PERSONAL RESPONSIBILITY	being aware of the part our thoughts, feelings and actions play in shaping our life and well-being. Then making a conscious choice to take a path that nourishes our well-being and contributes to our success
PROCESS	the moment-to-moment accumulation of action, thought and feeling unique to each individual and group. Process is dynamic, nebulous and alive
PUNISHMENT	the withholding or removal of desired objects, responses or relationships in return for certain behaviours and ways of being
RAPID CHANGE	a phenomena, that those of us living today are experiencing changes in our environment that are more rapid and radical than ever before
REAL	the quality of presence that people exhibit when relating from their ESSENTIAL YOU
REALITY	what is actually happening viewed from the clarity of ESSENTIAL YOU (therefore not distorted by WOUNDED YOU or DEFENDED YOU). Each person will see their own reality which will be true for them
RECOVERY MOVEMENT	programs and their supporting research to help people who are recovering from addictions such as alcoholism, drug addiction, overeating, workaholism and co-dependency
RELATIONSHIP	the ability to connect with another person as a human being. This usually requires the acknowledgement and acceptance of your own and the other person's DEFENDED YOU, WOUNDED YOU and ESSENTIAL YOU

REWARD	the giving of desired objects, responses or relationships in return for certain behaviours or ways of being
SAFE PEOPLE	people who create around them an environment in which each individual is encouraged, supported and validated for being real
SCAPEGOAT	someone found to carry the blame when events do not turn out according to plan
SELF	the essential and real part of a person equivalent to ESSENTIAL YOU
SELF-ACCEPTANCE	the ability to accept all the parts of ourselves without self-judgement
SELF-JUDGEMENT	the process of judging (often harshly) certain aspects of ourselves
SELF-LIMITING BELIEFS	beliefs about ourselves that get in the way of our achieving, experiencing and enjoying our full potential
SOCIALISATION	the process by which we learn to fit into the family and society in which we live
STAKEHOLDER	a person or group of people who directly or indirectly affect the way we make and enact decisions
STRATEGY	the direction and manner in which an individual or organisation intends to move forward into the future. Usually includes stated objectives and plans of action
STRATEGY IN MOTION	a dynamic on-going form of strategy formulation and implementation that takes account of the effects of rapid change, politics, relationship and human idiosyncrasy

STRATEGIC THINKING TIME	a mechanism for creating sufficient personal space to think effectively about 'strategy in motion'
UNAWARE/ UNCONSCIOUS	failing to acknowledge or accept our own thoughts, feeling or actions and the part they play in our lives
UNLEARNING	letting go old thoughts, feelings and behaviours that no longer contribute to our well–being and success
VALUE	a statement of what we hold to be important. A value can be personal and/or organisational
VISION	a statement of what we want to achieve. Most effectively stated as being time–bounded and in line with mission and values
WOUNDED YOU	is our vulnerable child–self, which consists of powerful and repressed feelings, both pleasant and unpleasant.

Bibliography

Cornelius, Helena and Faire Shoshana 1986, *Everyone Can Win*, Simon and Schuster, Australia.

Drucker, Peter 1985, *Innovation and Entrepreneurship*, Heinemann, London.

Dwyer, Wayne 1981, *Your Erroneous Zones*, Sphere Books, London.

Goldhor, Harriet 1989 *The Dance of Intimacy*, Harper and Row, New York.

Garland, Ron 1989, *Working and Managing in a New Age*, Wildwood House, Great Britain.

Gleick, James 1988, *Chaos*, Penguin Group, London.

Harville, Hendrix 1988, *Getting the Love you Want*, Schwartz and Wilkinson, Melbourne.

Iacocca, Lee 1984, *Iacocca*, Bantam Books, New York.

Johnson, Gerry *Managing Strategic Change, The Role of Strategic Formulation*, University of Aston, Birmingham.

Jampolsky, Gerald 1985 *Good Bye to Guilt*, Bantam Books, New York.

Kopp, Sheldon 1990, *If you Meet the Buddha on the Road, Kill Him!*, Sheldon Press, London.

Leider, Richard 1985, *The Power of Purpose*, Ballantine Books, New York.

Lowen, Alexander 1980, *Fear of Life*, Collier books, New York.

Miller, Alice 1989, *The Drama of Being a Child*, Virago Press, London.

Paul, Jordan and Margaret 1988, *From Conflict to Caring*, Compcare 1988, Minneapolis.

Peters, Thomas and Waterman, Robert 1982, *In Search of Excellence*, Harper and Row, New York.

Porter, Michael 1980, *Competitive Strategy*, The Free Press, New York.

Satir, Virginia 1972, *People Mating*, Science and Behaviour Books, Palo Alto.

Thoele, Sue Patton 1988, *The Courage to be Yourself, A Women's Guide to Growing Beyond Emotional Dependance*, Pyramid Press, Nevada City.

Whitfield, Charles 1987, *Healing the Child Within*, Health Communications Inc. Florida.

Whitfield, Charles 1990, *A Gift to Myself*, Health Communications Inc. Deerfield Beach, Florida